And Now You

50 NORTH AMERICAN NATIVE LEGENDS

John W. Friesen and Virginia Lyons Friesen

Copyright © 2009
John W. Friesen and Virginia Lyons Friesen

12 13 14 15 16   5 4 3 2

Excerpts from this publication may be reproduced under licence from Access Copyright, or with the express written permission of Brush Education Inc., or under licence from a collective management organization in your territory. All rights are otherwise reserved and no part of this publication may be reproduced, stored in a retrieval system, or transmitted in any form or by any means, electronic, mechanic, photocopying, digital copying, scanning, recording or otherwise, except as specifically authorized.

Brush Education Inc.
Calgary, Alberta, Canada
www.brusheducation.ca
contact@brusheducation.ca

Produced with the assistance of the Government of Alberta, Alberta Multimedia Development Fund. We also acknowledge the financial support of the Government of Canada through the Canada Book Fund for our publishing activities.

Library and Archives Canada
Cataloguing in Publication

Friesen, John W.
  And now you know : 50 north American native legends /
John W. Friesen, Virginia L. Friesen.
    ISBN 978-1-55059-384-6
  1. Indians of North America--Folklore. 2. Legends--North America.
I. Friesen, Virginia Lyons, 1952- II. Title.
  E98.F6F726 2010   398.2089'97   C2009-906739-0

Printed and manufactured in Canada.

Cover illustration: *Eagle Feather,* by David J. Friesen. Many North American Native people view the eagle feather as sacred. Traditionally, individuals were awarded with an eagle feather in recognition of a special gift or for a significant contribution to their community. An Elder might hold an eagle feather while instructing youth in cultural lore or relating a legend.

To honor our twelfth grandchild,
Andrew Jason Droppert
Born April 23, 2008

Contents

Part One: Origin Stories

Origin of Buffalo: A Sioux Legend · 15
Origin of Buffalo Hunting: A Mandan Legend · 17
Origin of Cherokee Rose: A Cherokee Legend · 19
Origin of Chief Mountain: A Peigan Legend · 21
Origin of Chinook Wind: A Salish Legend · 23
Origin of Corn: A Pueblo Legend · 25
Origin of Family Crests: A West Coast Legend · 29
Origin of Fire and Light: A Klamath Legend · 31
Origin of Fire: A Salish Legend · 33
Origin of Human Hands: A Chumash Legend · 35
Origin of the North Star (Star Boy): A Blackfeet Legend ·37
Origin of Obsidian Arrowheads: A Shasta Legend · 41
Origin of Orion's Belt: A Sioux Legend ·43
Origin of Raven's Cry: A Kwakwaka'waka Legend · 45
Origin of the Rocky Mountains: A Cree Legend · 47
Origin of Stone Woman: A Dakota Legend · 51
Origin of Turtle Island: A Wyandot Legend · 53
Origin of Turtles: A Mi'kmaq Legend · 55
Origin of Wild Rice: An Ojibway Legend · 57

Part Two: How Stories

How Birds Can be Teachers: A Pawnee Legend · 61
How Loon Became a Seabird: A Mi'kmaq Legend · 63
How to Call Moose: A Wabanaki Legend · 65
How Yellow Mouse Fooled Owl: A Creek Legend · 67
How Porcupine Got Quills: A Chippewa Legend · 69
How Spotted Eagle Earned His Feather: A Mohawk Legend · 71
How Whale Kept His Promise: A Haida Legend · 75

Part Three: Why Stories

Why Badger is Humble: An Interior Salish Legend · 79
Why Beaver is Respected: A Dene Legend · 81
Why Buzzards are Bald: An Algonquian Legend · 83
Why Coyote Looks at His Stomach: An Okanagan Legend · 85
Why Coyote's Eyes are Red: A Shuswap Legend · 87
Why Dogs Bark: A Kiowa Legend · 89
Why Eagle Went Hungry: A Sioux Legend · 91
Why Eagles Are Respected: An Iroquois Legend · 93
Why Fawn Has Spots: A Dakota Legend · 95

Why Moose Has Loose Skin: A Swampy Cree Legend · 97
Why Porcupine is Respected: A Tsimshian Legend · 99
Why Possum is Shy: A Creek Legend · 101
Why Rabbit Turns White in Winter: A Cree Legend · 103
Why Wolverine Has Short Legs: A Cree Legend · 105

Part Four: Ten Tricky Trickster Tales

Copycat Coyote and Rattlesnake: A Sia Legend · 109
Coyote and Magpie Go Hunting: A Thompson Legend · 111
Coyote and Quail: A Pima Legend · 113
Raven and the Magpies: A Tlinget Legend · 115
Coyote and Water Serpent: A Hopi Legend · 117
Coyote and Wild Turkey: An Algonquian Legend · 121
Napi, Skunk, and the Prairie Dogs: A Blackfoot Legend · 123
Raven Burns a Canoe: A West Coast Legend · 125
Raven Learns a Lesson: A Tsimshian Legend · 127
The Trickster and Eagle: An Assiniboine Legend · 129

Appendices

Appendix A · A Note On Terminology · 132
Appendix B · Interpreting Legends · 133
Appendix C · Native American Rock Art: Pictographs and Petroglyphs · 136
Appendix D · About the Authors · 144
Bibliography · 148

Introduction

BEFORE THE PRINTING PRESS dominated the world of formal communication, families, communities, and cultures all over the world relied solely on the oral tradition to pass along revered knowledge. Much valued cultural content, particularly spiritual or historical beliefs and practices, was transmitted through legends or stories shared between generations. This responsibility rested with formally acknowledged storytellers, as well as elders. This practice was very much the case with Aboriginal tribes in North America.

This collection of North American Aboriginal cultural stories represents only a small component of this vast store of oral literature, and underscores the magnitude of its scope across various Native American and Canadian Indian tribes.

Purpose of the Book

Legends contained in this volume have been drawn from a diverse store of written sources, documented in the bibliography. Through the years that we have been associated with the University of Calgary, we have visited most of the traditional tribal communities represented in this book. We have taught university courses in several First Nations communities including Blackfoot, Chipewyan, Plains Cree, Woodland Cree, Stoney (Nakoda Sioux), and Tsuu T'ina (Sarcee).

From time immemorial, Native Americans of all backgrounds have been oriented to the arts, which comprised an important cultural component. Each particular art form reflected the cultural makeup and physical resources of the region in which a tribe lived. Plains Indians, for example, relied heavily on rock art, consisting of paintings and carvings done on rocks. This art form is recognizable today in the form of pictographs and petroglyphs. A full explanation of the nature and function of this art form is offered in *Appendix C* at the back of the book.

The essence of each traditional Indigenous story contained in this volume has been preserved, although individual legends have in most cases been abbreviated from their original sources, and written in language that may readily be understood by and shared with children. It is also our hope that through this means would-be students of Indigenous ways may learn a great deal about Aboriginal culture and philosophy and, hopefully, enhance their respect for AmerIndian ways.

Acknowledgements

THIS WORK would not have been possible without the assistance, encouragement, and support of many individuals from a wide variety of backgrounds including:

◾ members of the various Native American communities we have visited over the past two decades from the four western Canadian provinces through the Dakotas to Arizona and Texas;

◾ members of the Stoney (Nakoda Sioux) First Nation with whom we have spent many happy years exchanging ideas and learning about their cultural history and spiritual beliefs and practices;

◾ students at the University of Calgary who have acknowledged the value of our courses in Aboriginal art, education, and Plains Indian history;

◾ Dr. Ted Giles (president), May Misfeldt, and other staff members of Temeron/Detselig, our favorite publishing firm;

◾ administrators of the Graduate Division of Educational Research and the Faculty of Communication and Culture at the University of Calgary, for providing facilities for us to pursue our research interests;

◾ our son, David J Friesen, who added to his workload at the Ashiya International School in Japan, to provide art work for this book; and, our children-Bruce, Karen, Gaylene, David, and Beth Anne — who have from time to time patiently listened to us elaborating on our travels and studies.

While we owe a great deal of thanks to these individuals and groups, we do acknowledge that the idea and content of this work was our idea, and we are honored to defend it. More than anything, it is our hope that this work will encourage the public to formulate an appreciation for and more meaningful understanding of First Nations history, spirituality, and culture.

J.W.F.
V.L.F.
University of Calgary
2009

Part One:
Origin Stories

Origin of Buffalo

A Sioux Legend

When the Great Spirit first created animals and the people of the plains, He did not create buffalo. They were created later.

At that time, the various Indian tribes who lived on the North American plains enjoyed eating nutritious roots, berries, and nuts, and also hunted small animals for food. The people lived a rich, full life, but one day the Creator came up with a new idea.

"I want to create a special animal for the people of the plains," the Creator announced one day. "It will be a superior animal, one that can provide everything for the people: warm clothing, delicious food, useful tools, and even thick teepee coverings to keep out the cold. The people will be able to make the horns and hooves of this special animal into useful items. The animal will be called buffalo, and he will have a very large hump on his back. He will be able to run very fast but he will have poor eyesight so that hunters will be able to trap him. That way the people can use the many gifts of the buffalo to enrich their lives."

The Creator went ahead with His plan and created the buffalo.

The North American plains are generally quite flat, and people can see for a long distances on the plains. In places, however, there are also small hills and even curvy valleys on the plains. As the Creator looked around for a good place for the buffalo to be born, He saw a deep valley with a large cave at the end. At once the Creator decided this would be a good place for the buffalo to be born.

One day, a plains tribe, the Sioux, decided to move to a new location near a series of rolling hills. One of the hills had a cave in it, and this is where the first buffalo came to the plains. A skilled Sioux hunter out hunting, was suddenly surprised as he watched the first burly buffalo emerge from the cave, followed by another and another and another. Soon the whole valley was full of heavy buffalo and they spread to the plains in large numbers. The Sioux hunter was amazed at what he saw. When he was finally able to catch his breath he ran back to his village and shared the wonderful news. The buffalo would be a good animal to provide food and clothing and useful utensils. By now a large herd of buffalo had also reached the village area and the people wondered where this magnificent animal had come from. The hunter who had first spied them was happy to tell his story.

Quickly, a group of village hunters prepared to go on a buffalo hunt. Before long the villagers were enjoying their first taste of buffalo meat. It did not take long for the Plains Indians of North America to discover the many other uses they could make of the "supermarket of the plains" – the buffalo. Soon the Plains Indians became known as buffalo people.

And now you know how buffalo came to be.

Origin of Buffalo Hunting

A Mandan Legend

The buffalo has long been important to the Plains Indians. Before people from Europe arrived in North America, Indian culture of the plains and prairies was built around this animal. The buffalo has been called "the supermarket of the plains," because it once provided for all the people's needs. Nutritious buffalo meat could be boiled, fried, or dried for later use. Thick buffalo hides were made into large teepees and warm clothing. Buffalo bones could be carved into tools, cooking utensils, and many other useful items. Indian people believe that the buffalo is a gift from the Creator.

Before buffalo hunting began, the First Nations of North America ate berries, roots, and nuts and hunted smaller animals and birds. Even though there were buffalo around, they could not be hunted because the animals were too large, too fast, and too smart to be trapped. Everyone wished they could hunt buffalo. Someone had once tasted buffalo meat and declared that it was very delicious and nourishing.

If you study buffalo today, you will discover that while they can run very fast, they do not have very good eyesight. This was not always the case. According to Mandan history, buffaloes used to have very good eyesight. They could spot a hunter a long ways off and when they did, they would run away. As a result, the Indian people could not have buffalo meat to eat.

One day Coyote, the trickster, felt sorry for the Mandan people. Although he often played tricks on others, Coyote could also do useful things if he felt like it. The trickster had power to do both good things or play tricks. This time Coyote wanted to do something good; he wanted the people to have buffalo meat, so this is what he did.

One day when a herd of buffalo came close to Coyote, he threw very fine sand in their eyes and

dimmed their eyesight. Now they could not see well. Then Coyote bent down the heads of the buffalo to make them hang closer to the ground. That way they would not always be able to see hunters sneaking up on them. Now it was possible for the Indians to hunt buffalo. Before long the Plains and prairie Indian way of life became known as a buffalo culture, thanks to the Coyote, the trickster.

And now you know how buffalo hunting began.

Origin of Cherokee Rose

A Cherokee Legend

These are the names of five great southeast Native American Indian tribes: Cherokees, Chickasaws, Creeks, Choctaws, and Seminoles. Today these five tribes are all friendly with one another, but in years gone by they were sometimes enemies.

ONE DAY, when two of the five tribes were at war with one another, it happened that the Cherokees took prisoner a brave Seminole warrior named Wolf Fighter. Since Wolf Fighter was their prisoner, the Cherokees wanted to inflict pain on him. However, in the meantime, Wolf Fighter turned very ill. The Cherokees did not believe in punishing a sick man, so they decided to nurse Wolf Fighter back to health first. A young woman named Rose was assigned to look after the young warrior, and she agreed to do so.

It took a long time for Wolf Fighter to regain his health, and each day Rose took care of him and provided for his needs. Rose would regularly put a cold cloth on Wolf Fighter's forehead to cool the temperature of his raging fever. She fed him root tea and warm soup. She kept blankets on him to keep him warm. Rose did everything an excellent nurse would do, and Wolf Fighter was very grateful. Once in a while a Cherokee warrior would come by Rose's wigwam to see how Wolf Fighter was getting along.

As the weeks passed by and Wolf Fighter was regaining his health, he and Rose had many opportunities to talk with one another. In fact, one day they realized that they had fallen in love. They also realized that Wolf Fighter would soon be well enough to be punished by the Cherokees. That is what the Cherokees did to their enemies.

Now that Rose had fallen in love with Wolf Fighter, she decided to save his life. She arranged for him to escape from the wigwam where he was held prisoner. However, he refused to leave unless Rose went with him. After much discussion, Rose agreed to go with Wolf Fighter, so when nightfall came the two of them together fled into the black darkness of the night.

The youthful pair had not gone far when Rose asked if she could return to her village to obtain a memento from her family home to take with her. She wanted something by which to remember her people. Wolf Fighter agreed with the idea, so Rose quietly retraced her steps to her family wigwam. Rose quickly picked one of the colorful roses that was blooming in her mother's garden. Then the two lovers were off again into the night fleeing to Wolf Fighter's people. After a long and tiresome journey, Wolf Fighter and Rose made it safely to Wolf Fighter's Seminole village.

Today lovely roses grow in Seminole country and they originated with the one flower that Rose brought with her that night. Today that beautiful and sweet-smelling flower is called Cherokee Rose.

And now you know how the Cherokee Rose originated.

Origin of Chief Mountain
A Peigan Legend

There was once a young Peigan warrior named Black Bear who was known for his bravery. Because of his mighty deeds, it did not take long before Black Bear became a respected war chief among his own people. One day he fell in love with a beautiful young woman and the two were married. The couple were very happy, and in due time they had a baby boy.

When the boy was still very young, a war party from an enemy tribe attacked the village, resulting in a fierce battle. Many Peigan people were killed or wounded in the battle. Consequently, Black Bear announced that the enemy would have to be punished. He assembled a large number of warriors and they prepared to launch a surprise attack on the enemy camp.

Black Bear's wife insisted on going with the warriors, but her husband refused to allow her to come along.

"If I do not come with you," Black Bear's wife insisted, "you will have an empty teepee when you return from battle."

Those words caused Black Bear great concern. He worried about the safety of his wife and child. He talked for a long time with his wife and managed to calm her down, and convince her not to go to battle with him. She finally agreed to remain in the village with the other wives and children.

Chief Black Bear and his warriors were successful in defeating the enemy, but Black Bear himself was killed in the battle. Taking the young chief's body with them, the Peigan warriors sadly headed back to their village. When the young wife learned that her husband had been killed in battle, she took her baby boy and snuck away from the village in the dark of night. She headed for a high mountain. The young wife climbed as high as she could. Then, overcome with grief, she took her baby in her arms, and jumped off the mountain. Both she and her baby fell to their death. When the villagers noticed that Black Bear's wife was missing, they began to look for her. Finally, after a long search they found her body and the body of the baby boy. They buried the young woman and her child at the base of the mountain.

Today this mountain is known as Chief Mountain. Chief Mountain is located in the U.S. state of Montana on the eastern border of Glacier National Park and the Blackfeet Indian Reservation. Local residents say that if you look really hard at the face of the mountain you will see the figure of the woman with the baby in her arms.

And now you know the sad story of naming Chief Mountain.

Origin of Chinook Wind
A Salish Legend

THUNDERBIRD is a large, powerful, mythical bird who, according to legend, lives on the West Coast of Canada. A long time ago, Thunderbird lived close, but not in the same area as the Salish people of British Columbia. The Salish people lived in a beautiful valley, completely surrounded by lush green grasses and colorful flowers. Thunderbird lived nearby in a very private area, an area that Coyote, the trickster, was not allowed to enter. Coyote and Thunderbird were not friends, and they did not speak to one another.

Thunderbird had three daughters: Blue Jay, Crow, and Magpie, and she was very proud of them. Each of her daughters had a special talent, but Blue Jay was the bravest of them.

Everyone was extremely happy for a time, but then something happened to change things. One day, a careless Salish hunter left his campfire unattended and fire from the glowing embers spread. The fire jumped from tree to tree, eventually reaching Thunderbird's home, and immediately burning it to the ground. Thunderbird was very upset. Everything was ruined. The green forest was badly burned, grass became blackened, and there were no flowers or berry bushes to be found anywhere.

Thunderbird was so angry that she flapped her huge wings and ordered the Salish people to leave the area. "Drive away the people who have destroyed my country," Thunderbird roared. Then she asked North Wind to blow across the valley.

North Wind descended on the valley where the people lived and the people began to shiver with cold. Heavy snows fell, and frightened animals went into hiding. Food became scarce.

Eventually Thunderbird's anger softened, and she asked North Wind to stop blowing. The wind stopped but the drifts of snow remained on the ground. Nothing could grow.

In the meantime, the people approached the trickster to help matters, but Coyote's response was, "Let the big bird with the loud noise take care of things. She ordered North Wind to come, so if the people do not have food that is not my problem."

One of Thunderbird's daughters, Blue Jay, decided to do something about the problem. She prayed to the Creator and asked for a soft, gentle wind that would melt the ice and snow and warm things up. The Creator called on Chinook Wind for help. Chinook Wind's heart was kind and warm, and Chinook Wind was always willing to help. Because of Blue Jay's request, the Creator asked Chinook Wind to melt the snow and warm up the area.

Soon Chinook Wind blew her warm, moist breath across the valley and without delay everything started to come to life again. The snow and ice melted, grass began to grow, and flowers bloomed. Deer, rabbits, and birds returned to their places, and everyone was happy again. The people were very grateful to Blue Jay and Chinook Wind. Even today, people in Salish country enjoy the warm soft wind of Chinook Wind.

And now you know and perhaps can appreciate the power of Chinook Wind.

Origin of Corn
A Pueblo Legend

Long, long ago, there were few people on earth. There was a scattering of North American southwest Indian villages, but none were heavily populated. Some people lived only with their families and some even lived by themselves.

There was one young Indian hunter named Grey Fox, who did not live in a village. He preferred to live by himself. Grey Fox's home was far away from the rest of the people. Though he was sometimes lonely, he seldom ventured into the villages. In those days everyone lived on roots, berries, nuts, and small game. They did not grow crops for food. Like his neighbors, Grey Fox did not have fire or meat, so he lived on roots, tree bark, nuts, and other foods.

One day, Grey Fox was napping beneath the shade of a large tree branch, and he woke to find what he thought was a creature in the distance moving towards him. For a moment it looked like another person. Then Grey Fox looked again, and sure enough, there was a human being coming closer to him.

Soon a beautiful young maiden stood before the Grey Fox. The woman looked unlike anyone the hunter had ever met before. She had long, light silken hair and a shy smile on her face. Grey Fox beckoned for the young maiden to come closer, but she would not. When Grey Fox tried to get a bit closer to the woman, she furtively backed away, so he followed her. Grey Fox began to speak to the woman and tell her how lonely he was but she did not answer immediately. After a long while, the maiden responded to the young hunter.

"If you follow me," she said, "I will never leave you. I will always stay with you." The hunter did not understand what she meant, but he eagerly began to follow her.

Soon the pair came to a clearing in the forest where there was a field of very dry grass. The maiden told Grey Fox to find two dry sticks and rub them together. He did so and before long, the sticks burst into flame. The maiden told Grey Fox to fan the flames into a real fire and then burn the field of dry grass. Grey Fox did as he was told.

When the grass was burned up, the maiden told Grey Fox to take her by the hair and drag her across the now parched field. Grey Fox did not quite understand why the woman would want him to do this, but she insisted, so he did as she asked. The maiden explained that if Grey Fox did what she requested, she would provide the people with a new food. She explained that new green plant shoots would grow into tall plants and produce seeds that would provide food. Grey Fox did not particularly like the idea; it seemed harsh, but the maiden was very persistent, so he reluctantly did as she said.

As the young hunter dragged the maiden along the ground, green shoots of small plants did appear behind her, and soon green leaves appeared on them- just as the maiden had predicted. The woman also told Grey Fox that he would see long thin strings of her hair appear among the green leaves. They would be wrapped around cobs of yellow seeds that would later appear. Everything happened just as the young woman said it would. Soon after the predicted little green shoots of plants appeared, the maiden disappeared.

Grey Fox discovered that when the strange new plants had grown tall, they bore yellow cobs of seed. The maiden had instructed that the seeds could be cooked, dried, and eaten. The new plant, of course, was corn, and that is how corn came to be.

Today, if you look closely at a corn plant you can see the young maiden's silken hair at the top of the ears of corn. This woman was the corn maiden, who brought new food to the Pueblo people.

So now you know how corn originated.

Origin of Family Crests
A West Coast Legend

Many North West Coast Indian tribes have family crests that are carved out of wood. A family crest is a symbol — much like a badge of honor. Some crest designs include beavers, birds (like Thunderbird), frogs, insects, mountain goats, sea otters, and whales. Sometimes plants or celestial bodies — sun, moon, and stars — are used on crests as well. For example, when Killer Whale is implanted on a crest it acknowledges that he is lord of the ocean and strong spirit of the sea.

Use of crests first occurred many generations ago, and they are handed down from one generation to the next. Individuals who receive a family crest are entitled to use the songs and dances that belong to it.

Crests used to be obtained through marriage or traded. In the past they were sometimes awarded as compensation, or obtained by defeating an enemy. Even today, many West Coast families proudly display their family crests in their homes or at important occasions.

The design for crests originated in different ways, and the origin can often be traced through a legend.

THERE WAS ONCE A BOY named Small Tree, who was not a particularly healthy boy. Sometimes he felt sad because he could not run or jump as well as the other boys in his tribe. In fact, he was not very good at any sport. As a result, Small Tree did not join in games when other boys played, but instead went off by himself. He did not want the other boys to make fun of his poorly developed skills.

One day Small Tree was standing on the shore of the Pacific Ocean when he heard a strange voice. He went closer to where the sound of the voice originated, and to his surprise, he saw a giant frog. Frog beckoned Small Tree to get on his back. Small Tree did so. Once on board, Frog dove into the ocean and took Small Tree down to Whale's home. Whale took an instant liking to the young boy and told him he would share a great secret with him. Whale said that if Small Tree would listen to him, he would give him strength and wisdom. Then, when Small Tree returned home, the people of his village would respect him. Small Tree spent the next few years learning about life in the sea and discovering the power of sea animals. Even though he was given many difficult tasks to perform, he always persevered.

One day Whale showed Small Tree how to make crests out of wood. He also gave him permission to use representations of the creatures of the sea on crests: Sea Bear, Sea Otter, Whale, and others. Soon after, Small Tree returned to the earth and shared his experiences with the families in his village. Soon many families began making crests to represent the themes of their family lines. Now everyone respected Small Tree, and eventually he was made chief of his village.

And now you know how family crests originated.

Origin of Fire and Light

A Klamath Legend

Fire is essential to all living creatures, including people and animals. Fire gives light, which makes day and night possible. It also provides warmth, and assists people in cooking delicious hot meals. There are many stories about how fire and light came to the people, and in nearly every story there is an account of someone stealing it.

In the Klamath version of the origin of fire and light, the sky people had both, but they did not want to share these elements with the people on earth. Because of this, there was little light on earth and it was also very cold. The people knew that fire could provide both light and warmth, but there was little they could do about it.

R<small>AVEN, THE TRICKSTER</small>, had traveled to the sky and found that the sky people had both fire and light. When Raven returned to earth and told everyone what he had seen, several creatures got together to try to do something about the situation. Eagle, Pigeon, Sandpiper, Hummingbird, and Water Ant held a council and devised a plan by which to steal fire and light from the sky people. Raven was also a member of the council. After much discussion, a plan was finally created and the group traveled upwards until they reached the home of the sky people. When they got there, Raven knocked on the door, but no one answered the door.

Raven then decided to disguise himself as a beautiful sky woman in order not to attract attention. He tied back his long hair, took his blanket, a burden basket filled with pitch and alder bark made to look like acorns and salmon, and a basket dipper. He certainly looked ready for his special role. Then, when no one was watching, Raven quietly slipped into sky country through a small side entrance.

The sky people were feasting when Raven arrived,

so they were too busy to notice his arrival. Besides, Raven's disguise made him fit in with the group extremely well. Raven saw two baskets hanging in the banquet hall — one filled with fire and the other with daylight. The feast went on until the wee hours of the morning, and just before daylight when everyone was sleepy, Raven grabbed the two baskets and ran. Suddenly the weary sky people realized what had happened and began to chase him. Raven quickly passed the baskets to Eagle who passed them to Pigeon, who passed them to Sandpiper, who passed them to Hummingbird. Then Hummingbird gave them to Water Ant who dove under water with them — holding the fire and light in his closed mouth.

As Water Ant emerged from the water, he opened his mouth and the fire caused the earth to burst into warmth and light. Soon there was fire for warmth and daylight everywhere.

And now you know how the Klamath people got fire and light.

Origin of Fire

A Salish Legend

LONG AGO there were two worlds, one here on earth and the other in the sky. Unfortunately, the only place that had fire was the upper world in the sky. The animals and people on earth wished they had fire. Sometimes it got very cold down on earth. It was also very dark. The animals and Salish people thought it would be good to have fire.

The animals held a council to decide how to get fire. They talked about it at length. They decided that the animal with the best war song should go to the upper world and get fire. Muskrat sang his war song first, followed by Wolf, Bear, and Fox. It was hard to decide which one to choose. Then the animals heard another creature singing his war song, but he was not part of the council. Wolf went to find out who was singing, and found that it was Coyote, the trickster. Coyote was sitting with his friend, Wren, who had a bow and some arrows with him.

The council asked Coyote to sing his song again, and he did so. All the animals immediately liked Coyote's war song, so the council decided that Coyote should go to get fire. Now the question was, how would Coyote get to the upper world? Wren suggested that he would shoot arrows into the sky to make a ladder. Then Coyote could climb the ladder and bring fire back to earth.

Wren shot arrows up into the sky and a ladder was quickly formed. Wren, being the lightest weight, climbed up the ladder and sent down a rope to make the ladder stronger. Now everyone was excited. Finally, they were going to get fire. The animals were so excited they all decided to climb the ladder and reach the upper world. Beaver climbed up, followed by Wolf, Fox, and Coyote.

Everything went well until Bear climbed the ladder. Bear himself was heavy enough, but he also took two large baskets of food with him so he would not be hungry. Bear was halfway up the ladder when it broke because of his weight. Bear was simply too heavy for the ladder. Bear fell down crashing to the ground, and the ladder was broken. Now no one else could climb the ladder.

The animals who had climbed the ladder to the upper world kept on with their plan to get fire. In the upper world, Keeper was the guardian of the fire. Keeper did not want to share the fire, so the animals had to find a way to get it from him. Coyote decided that Beaver should steal the fire.

The plan was that Beaver would jump into the river near Keeper's house and float down the river, pretending he was dead. Keeper would likely try to trap Beaver for his soft fur, and that would distract Keeper. While Beaver was doing all of this, Eagle would fly over to Keeper's house and land on the roof. He would pretend he was wounded and give Keeper something else to think about. While all of this was going on, Coyote would steal the fire.

The plan almost worked. However, at the last minute, Keeper saw that Coyote was trying to steal the fire. Quickly he sent Spider to make a net to catch Coyote. Four times Spider spun a web, but each time Coyote managed to escape. When Coyote reached the rope that held the broken ladder, he and the other animals slid down the rope back to earth with the fire. Happily, they all made it safely back to earth.

When Keeper saw that the animals on earth had fire he ordered rain to fall and put the fire out. The animals huddled over the fire, protecting it from the wet rain. The plan worked; they were able to keep fire, and they have it to this day.

And now you know how the Salish people got fire.

Origin of Human Hands
A Chumash Legend

A LONG TIME AGO, there was a great flood and water covered all of the earth. After the flood there were only animals living on earth. There were no people.

One day the Creator told the animals that He wanted to make people. He wanted to know what the animals thought people should look like.

Soon thereafter, some of the animals got together to decide what people should look like. Coyote (the trickster), Sun, Moon, Morning Star, Lizard, and Eagle held a council to decide on the matter. After some discussion, the group agreed on what people's faces, bodies, arms and legs should look like, but they could not decide on the shape of people's hands.

Eagle and Coyote kept arguing about the shape of hands that people should have. Eagle wanted people to have claws like he had, but wily Coyote insisted that people should have hands that looked like his paws. Coyote was very proud of his paws and he thought that people would be happy to have hands shaped like his paws.

There were a few other animals at the council meeting. One of them was Lizard, but he did not say anything. Coyote seemed to have a lot to say, so no one else had a chance to speak.

Eventually Coyote won his argument that people's hands should be shaped like his paws. The council also decided that the next day they would gather around a large, smooth, beautiful, soft, white rock and make an imprint of a hand on it.

Coyote was very excited, and he was just about to put his paw onto the rock when Lizard came up behind him and quickly stuck his toe print on the rock. Now Lizard's toe print was on the rock, and it was too late for anyone to do anything about it.

Coyote was furious and took off after Lizard, who

dove into a deep crack in the earth. Coyote was too large to fit in the crack, and he could not follow Lizard. After thinking about it, Eagle, Sun, and Moon thought Lizard's toe print was just right for people's handprint, and they approved of what Lizard had done. There was really nothing that Coyote could do about it. Just think; if Lizard had not done what he did, people today would have paws like Coyote.

And now you know why our hands look more like the toes of Lizard than the paws of Coyote.

Origin of the North Star (Star Boy)

A Blackfeet Legend

If you look carefully into the morning sky (or late at night), you will see a special star that rises in the prairie sky early each day. Today we call this the North Star (or Polaris), but the Blackfeet Indians know it as Star Boy. This is the story of Star Boy.

MANY MOONS AGO, there was a beautiful young Blackfeet maiden named Blue Cloud. Each morning, Blue Cloud would watch Morning Star rise and grace the heavens with his bright presence. Blue Cloud was so impressed that over time she fell in love with Morning Star. Blue Cloud was sure that one day Morning Star would love her as well, so she turned down each of the young men in the village who asked to marry her.

Then, sure enough, it happened. One day, Morning Star stood in the doorway of Blue Cloud's teepee and spoke to her. Of course, Blue Cloud did not recognize him because he looked much like all of the young men from the village.

"I am Morning Star," the young man said. "Each morning I look for you when I rise, and I have loved you from the first time I saw you." Blue Cloud was very excited, and the two of them were married shortly after that.

Morning Star took Blue Cloud to the sky to meet his parents, Sun and Moon. They welcomed her and gave her and Morning Star their own home to live in.

One day Moon spoke to Blue Cloud and said, "Here is a turnip digging stick for you to use. Turnips provide good food. You can dig up all kinds of turnip roots with this digging stick, but do not dig up the Large Turnip that sits just outside your house."

Blue Cloud thanked Moon for the digging stick and returned home, eager to use the new tool the next day.

Some time later, Blue Cloud and Morning Star had a son and named him Star Boy, after his father. Blue Cloud took good care of her baby boy and often went outside their house to dig turnip roots for supper. She always took Star Boy with her. She was also careful not to touch the Large Turnip that grew near her house, even though she was curious about it.

One day her curiosity was just too much, and Blue Cloud decided to dig up the Large Turnip just to see what was under it. She called four times for some cranes to help her dig, and they did as she asked. With the help of the cranes, Blue Cloud managed to roll the turnip over. Underneath where the Large Turnip had been, Blue Cloud saw a hole in the sky. It was the very hole by which she herself had been admitted to the sky. Blue Cloud peered through the hole in the sky and saw the village of her people – the Blackfeet – far below. Suddenly she felt very lonely and wished she could visit her people again.

When Sun and Moon discovered that Blue Cloud had disobeyed them and dug up the Large Turnip, they told Morning Star to send his wife and baby back to her people. It was a sad day when Blue Cloud and Star Boy were returned to earth. Morning Star refused to allow Blue Cloud to remain in the sky even though she begged him too.

"You have disobeyed the rules," Morning Star said quietly but firmly, "and you cannot live in the sky anymore." The couple both wept as Blue Cloud returned to the camp of the Blackfeet.

As Star Boy grew up he developed an unsightly scar on his face, and none of the village maidens would marry him. One particular girl he loved very much would not have anything to do with him because of the scar. After she rejected him, Star Boy became a wanderer.

While traveling around one day, Star Boy saw a bright trail leading up to the sky and he followed it. When he reached the sky, he met a wise, mysterious medicine woman who told him that the scar on his face had been put there by his grandfather, Sun, and only Sun could remove it. A short time later, Star Boy met Sun, but Sun did not recognize him. Then Star Boy met his father, Morning Star, and Morning Star did recognize Star Boy. Morning Star took Star Boy to Sun and told him it was his grandson, Star Boy. Then, after much coaxing, Sun took the scar off Star Boy's face. Star Boy then returned to earth to court the pretty maiden who had rejected him and she agreed to marry him. After a beautiful wedding they lived a very happy life together.

Morning Star eventually invited Star Boy and his bride to come and live with him in the sky and they did so. In fact, on a clear night you can see both Morning Star and Star Boy in the sky. Each morning, Star Boy rises first, followed by Morning Star, and then the Sun. Star Boy, who is sometimes called North Star, appears never to move. The other stars appear to move around him. Late in the evening and first thing in the morning, look up to the sky and you will see Star Boy: the North Star.

And now you know the origin of the North Star.

Origin of Obsidian Arrowheads
A Shasta Legend

When the Indians of California first started hunting, they used pine-bark points for arrowheads and spear points. They did not know about obsidian, which is a special kind of volcanic rock. Obsidian rock can be chipped to make very sharp points for arrowheads and spears.

It happened that Ground Squirrel was the only one who knew where to find the special rock that could be used to make strong, sharply-pointed arrowheads. Old Man Obsidian had lots of it, but he did not want to share it with anyone.

One day Ground Squirrel went to Old Man Obsidian with a basket of roots and offered to trade the roots for some obsidian. Old Man Obsidian liked the roots, but said he wanted more roots before he would trade. Ground Squirrel went off to find more roots.

When Ground Squirrel returned to Old Man Obsidian's lodge he discovered that the roots he had originally brought were all gone. He could not believe his eyes. "Have you eaten them all?" he asked Old Man Obsidian.

"No," said the old man. "Grizzly Bear came along and ate them. Now I need even more of them before I will trade with you."

Ground Squirrel went off hunting for more roots, and Old Man Obsidian followed him. Just when Ground Squirrel's basket was filled with roots, Grizzly Bear came along. He seized the roots from Ground Squirrel's basket and quickly ate them all. This made Old Man Obsidian angry. He desperately wanted those roots. Then Old Man Obsidian threw a sharp piece of obsidian at Grizzly Bear and killed him.

Ground Squirrel went off to gather more roots and accompanied Old Man Obsidian to his home to cook and eat the roots. There were enough roots for both of them. The next morning, Ground Squirrel began to moan loudly. He told Old Man Obsidian that he had eaten too many roots and he was very sick. Ground Squirrel was not really sick; he was just pretending.

Old Man Obsidian went into the woods to get some wood to make a fire and cook some broth for Ground Squirrel. The broth would make Ground Squrrel feel better. After Old Man Obsidian left, Ground Squirrel took all the obsidian points he could find in the lodge and headed for home. When Old Man Obsidian returned to his lodge and discovered that his obsidian points were gone, he chased after Ground Squirrel. Just as Old Man Obsidian spied Ground Squirrel, he quickly dove into a burrow, which was connected to a long tunnel that led to the far side of a lake. When Ground Squirrel emerged safely from the tunnel on the other side of the lake, he found his people and gave them the obsidian points.

For many days the people worked to replace the pine-bark points on their arrowheads with obsidian points. Now they would be more successful hunters. They were very grateful to Ground Squirrel for bringing them the sharp rock points.

And now you know how the people got obsidian arrowheads.

Origin of Orion's Belt

A Sioux Legend

There were once two brothers, Left Rib and Walks Tall, who were great hunters. The two brothers spent many days on the prairies searching for game to provide food for their families.

Left Rib's wife, Golden Fawn, stayed at home with their son, Little Fox, but she wanted to see more of the world. She even asked to go hunting with the two brothers, but they refused to take her along.

One day Golden Fawn was so bored she decided to play a trick on the brothers. She put a pair of antelope horns on her head and snuck into the forest where her husband and his brother were hunting. Then she hid in some bushes and slowly stuck the antelope horns out of the bushes.

When the two brothers saw the antelope horns they rushed over to the place where they saw what they thought was an antelope. To their surprise, when the brothers arrived at the place they found Golden Fawn. When Golden Fawn saw the brothers coming, she quickly took off the antelope horns.

Left Rib and Walks Tall were surprised to see her. "Did you see an antelope pass by here?" they asked Golden Fawn.

"Oh yes," said Golden Fawn. "It was a very large antelope, but you are too late. It scurried off into the forest." Quickly the brothers entered the forest in the direction Golden Fawn was pointing, hoping to see the antelope.

The next day and the one that followed, Golden Fawn played the same trick on the brothers. In the evening the brothers would gather their friends around the fire and tell them about the great antelope they kept missing. Golden Fawn could hardly keep from laughing.

One day the two brothers decided to hunt separately. That way they would have a better chance of finding the mysterious antelope. Walks Tall went on ahead and Left Rib followed a long way behind. Suddenly Left Rib saw his wife, Golden Fawn, sneaking along quietly with antelope horns on her head. Left Rib realized that it was her playing a trick him and his brother. Left Rib did not tell Golden Fawn that he had seen her. Instead, he decided to play a trick on her.

The next day Left Rib told Golden Fawn that he would look after Little Fox so she could go berry picking. Then Left Rib and Walks Tall took Little Fox and followed Golden Fawn to where she was berry picking. All three of them put antelope horns on their heads and made sure that Golden Fawn could see them. When she saw the antelope horns, Golden Fawn ran home to get a bow and some arrows. She was going to shoot the three antelope and make a big feast.

Golden Fawn ran quickly to the place where she had seen the three sets of antelope horns worn by Left Rib, Walks Tall and Little Fox. As she got closer, the three of them ran and she began to chase them.

Soon Golden Fawn saw that each antelope had only two legs. She was shocked. With a screech of anger, she bolted after them and disappeared over a hill: right into the sky!

Today, on a clear night you can look up to the sky and see a row of three stars with a fourth star following them. The Sioux say this is the two brothers and Little Fox being chased by Golden Fawn. All of them ran so hard they ran right into the sky. That is why the stars are the way they are. Scientists call this constellation, Orion's Belt.

And now you know how Orion's Belt originated.

Origin of Raven's Cry
A Kwakwaka'waka Legend

RAVEN, THE TRICKSTER, had four cousins—Blue Jay, Crow, Squirrel, and Snail. All of them were very hard workers. During the summer, the four cousins picked large quantities of berries and preserved them for the long cold winter ahead. They also smoked, dried, and stored clams, which happen to be one of Raven's favorite foods.

When Raven found out about the food his cousins had prepared, he came up with a plan to steal the food. He invited his cousins to a council and made a suggestion, "Why don't we take some of this fine food you have gathered to the village and share it with the people? That would be a true gesture of good will."

Raven's cousins agreed that this was a good idea. They borrowed a large canoe from a neighbor, and loaded it with berries and clams to take to the village. As the four cousins prepared to leave for the village, Raven climbed into the canoe with them. Soon the five of them were paddling off on the lake toward the village.

The group had not gone far when Raven announced that he wanted to get out of the boat to take a break.

"Paddle over to the shore," he announced. "I want to take a brief walk. I will only be gone for a little while."

When the canoe reached the shoreline, Raven stepped out of the canoe and went to hide behind some bushes. Then he began to make weird noises that sounded like many warriors approaching.

He returned to his cousins waiting in the canoe and said, "Did you hear the loud noises? I think an army of warriors is coming to attack us. You four go and hide in the trees and I will remain here. If they see that I am the only one here, they will probably not harm me."

Without thinking and somewhat scared, the cousins did as Raven suggested. Blue Jay, Crow, and Squirrel quickly got out of the canoe and ran to shore, but Snail was much slower. Impatiently, Raven grabbed Snail and threw her out of the canoe into the water. Then he started to eat the berries and clams as fast as he could.

When Snail recovered from being thrown into the water, she realized what Raven was doing. She called to the other cousins and told them that Raven was eating all their food. The cousins quickly came out of their hiding places, swam over to the canoe and grabbed the canoe paddles. Then they began beating Raven with the paddles. Raven began shouting with pain, "Don't, don't, don't, don't," and that is the cry of the Raven to this day.

And now you know the origin of Raven's cry!

Origin of the Rocky Mountains:
A Cree Legend

BIG MAN, a man of great stature, was one of the very largest men who ever lived. Normally, teepees are covered with ten to twelve buffalo hides, but his teepee was so large it took more than one hundred buffalo hides to cover it. The dish that Big Man ate out of was larger than a canoe and one meal for him was a moose, two deer, and fifty partridges!

Everyone who knew Big Man feared him because not only was he big, he was known as a mean man. Sometimes Big Man did not watch where he was walking and he stepped on smaller creatures. At times he even stepped on people. One day he snuck into a Cree camp and snatched an orphan boy named Red Feather. Then Big Man made Red Feather his slave.

Red Feather had to live in Big Man's teepee and do a lot of chores. Fortunately, he was able to make a friend who also lived in the teepee, a moose named Swift Foot.

Big Man traveled a lot. He had been to the plains, the northern regions, and the woodland country. However, he had not gone too far west because he heard there was a man who lived there named Great Rock. It was said that Great Rock was even bigger than Big Man.

Whenever Big Man was off traveling, Red Feather and Swift Foot played together and had good times. Swift Foot told Red Feather that someday he would help Red Feather escape from Big Man's teepee.

One day Big Man announced that he was going on a long trip. After he left, Swift Foot said to Red Feather, "Today we will escape from Big Man's teepee. You will climb on my back and we will travel fast. Be sure to bring a clod of earth, a piece of moss, a stone, and the branch of a tree with you."

Red Feather did as he was told, but he wondered why he had to bring all those things with him.

Swift Foot assured him that he would find out soon enough.

They had traveled only a short distance when they noticed Big Man coming after them, riding on a great caribou.

"Quickly throw out your clod of earth," Swift Foot cried, and Red Feather did so. Immediately a series of hills rose up behind them and it took Big Man many days to cross the hills. Soon he was behind them and catching up again.

"Fling out your piece of moss," cried Swift Foot, as the two of them ran, and Red Feather did so. Quickly, a muskeg swamp appeared behind the two and Big Man and his great caribou became mired in the swamp. Big Man eventually made it through the sludge and was again gaining on the escaping pair.

When Swift Foot and Red Feather saw Big Man advancing on them Swift Foot commanded, "Fling out the stone you are carrying," and Red Feather did so. This time a range of high, jagged looking mountains appeared that were heavily covered with snow and icy glaciers. This time it looked as though Big Man would never catch them, but the fugitives were wrong. After many days, Big Man was close behind them again. For the fourth time, Swift Foot cried out to Red Feather, "Fling out the tree branch you brought with you," and Red Feather did so.

Immediately there arose a mighty forest behind them with trees so thick that Big Man could not pass among them. Determined to finally cut his way through, Big Man struggled hard, but his great caribou got his antlers stuck in the branches while trying to escape. Leaving the great caribou behind, Big Man scrambled madly toward them.

As Big Man came closer, Swift Foot quickly helped Red Feather across a wide, wide river. This was the mighty Yukon River. Without his great caribou, Big Man was not able to follow the two escapees across the river. Big Man could not swim, and the great caribou was stuck back in the forest.

Big Man demanded Red Feather help him across the river, but instead Swift Foot offered to do so. When Big Man and Swift Foot were halfway across the river, Swift Foot dropped Big Man into the swirling current. Big Man was swiftly swept down stream and never seen again.

Today all that is left of this adventure are the Rocky Mountains in North America, stretching from the Alberta and British Columbia border southward to the American State of New Mexico.

And now you know how the Rocky Mountains came to be.

50

Origin of Stone Woman
A Dakota Legend

A LONG TIME AGO, Black Eagle, a Dakota warrior, married Pretty Feather, a women from the Arikara tribe who lived further north. The couple moved to the Dakota village and everything seemed to go well. Black Eagle and Pretty Feather had a son, and they were very happy. Pretty Feather's relatives did not live too far away and she occasionally went to visit them.

One day Black Eagle and the other villagers decided to move to another location. They thought that the hunting would be better in their new surroundings. There would be fishing opportunities there as well because of the many deep, beautiful lakes nearby and full of fish.

The day of the move arrived and everyone packed up their teepees and belongings. Family goods were loaded onto travois and horses were saddled up.

When Black Eagle came to his teepee to see if Pretty Feather was ready, he found that she was not packing up her goods.

"I am not moving," Pretty Feather told Black Eagle. "I like it here. This place is closer to my people and I do not want to leave." Pretty Feather held her baby close and refused to budge.

After coaxing and begging his wife to come with them, Black Eagle and his neighbors decided to move on. They were sure that Pretty Feather would change her mind and follow them, but she did not.

They had not gone far when Black Eagle began to worry. "How would his wife take care of herself? Who would provide food for her and their baby?"

He spoke to his two brothers. "Why don't the two of you go back and plead with Pretty Feather to come with us? Maybe you will have better luck convincing her to come than I did. Maybe she will listen to you."

The two brothers did as requested and rode back to the village site. They saw Pretty Feather, their sister-in-law sitting alone, holding her baby.

"Sister-in-law, we have come to get you. The tribe is waiting for you. Please get up and join us," they pleaded.

Then one of the brothers put his hand on Pretty Feather's shoulder, then lightly touched her head. It was hard and cold. Then he discovered that after the tribe had left Pretty Feather and the baby had both turned to stone.

The brothers returned to Black Eagle and told him what had happened. Immediately the villagers went back to the place where they had once camped and saw a block of stone in the form of a woman and her child.

For years afterward the unique stone was called Stone Woman, and the people took Stone Woman with them whenever they moved camp. The statue was always placed in the center of the camp. It was considered sacred to the people.

Today you can see the statue of Stone Woman in front of the Standing Rock Indian Agency in South Dakota.

And now you know how Stone Woman originated.

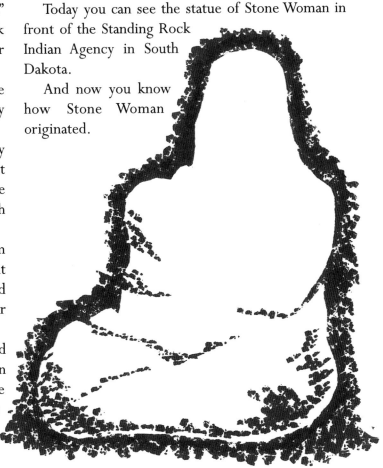

Origin of Turtle Island
A Wyandot Legend

The Wyandot people believe that the universe consists of two levels — an upper world, and a lower world. The upper world is in the sky and the lower world is the earth. The Wyandot also believe that their people once lived in the upper world, while animals and birds occupied the lower world, which was mainly covered with water.

The story of how the Wyandot people began to live in the lower world begins with a family of brothers and sisters who lived together in the upper world. It was a world that did not change. Day after day family members did the same things and had the same food to eat. Gradually, they grew tired of their menu, which consisted only of corn. Each day the brothers and sisters picked a basketful of corn and ate it. The next day they did exactly the same thing. It was not a very exciting way to get food, and the family was quite weary of their corn diet.

One day, one of the sisters decided to break the routine by cutting down all the stalks of corn in the garden. Unfortunately, the garden was now destroyed and there was no food to eat. The brothers were so furious that they dropped their sister down to the lower world through a hole in the sky.

A flock of geese floating on the water in the lower world saw the woman fall to earth. Quickly the geese moved into place so the woman landed on their backs. Unhurt by the fall, the woman remained on the backs of the geese for a long while. Gradually the geese began to get very tired. Then, suddenly Turtle appeared and offered to take a turn holding the woman. He was very large and very strong and easily kept the woman out of the surrounding water.

Toad saw all of this and dove down beneath the waters, returning with a handful of mud for the woman. He instructed the woman to sprinkle the mud around. As she did so, the mud turned into land. Soon there was a large piece of land located on the back of the turtle. The woman got up and began to walk around the land. More people joined her, and since that time the Wyandot people have lived on the land. That land came to be called Turtle Island, and today everyone is living on it.

And now you know how Turtle Island originated.

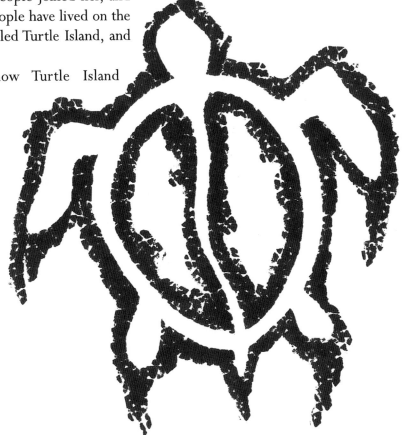

Origin of Turtles
A Mi'kmaq Legend

One day Glooscap came to a Mi'kmaq village to see his people. He decided to stay with Big Eagle, an old man whom he had known for a long time. Big Eagle was always hospitable to Glooscap and Glooscap enjoyed staying in Big Eagle's wigwam.

While he was visiting Big Eagle, Glooscap discovered that Big Eagle loved a pretty maiden named Cornflower. Cornflower did not want anything to do with Big Eagle, because he was too old and too poor. Glooscap felt sorry for Big Eagle so he used his magic to make Big Eagle young and handsome. Then Big Eagle went to Cornflower's father and asked for her hand in marriage. Cornflower's father agreed and so did Cornflower. Big Eagle looked so young and handsome. Soon a wedding date was set.

When the young men in the village heard that Cornflower was going to marry Big Eagle, they were very angry with Glooscap for making Big Eagle young again. They even threatened to harm Glooscap, but they did not know that Glooscap had special power.

When the wedding feast was announced, two of the angry young men seated themselves next to Glooscap, intending to hurt him. Glooscap had heard the men talking, so he was ready for them. When the meal was over, Glooscap got up and touched both of the angry young two men on their noses, and made their noses completely flat. The men did not find this out until later, and when they did they hid themselves and were not seen much after that. One of the men became Toad and the other became Porcupine. Those animals both have flat noses to this day.

There were two other young men who were angry that Glooscap had made Big Eagle young again, but Glooscap knew their plan. Part of the marriage festival included a game in which everyone was invited to take part. When these two jealous men participated, they threw Big Eagle very high to the top of a wigwam and he could not get down.

When Glooscap saw what had happened, he went into the wigwam and smoked his pipe all night. The smoke reached Big Eagle at the top of the wigwam, and turned his skin hard and wrinkled. Glooscap then turned Big Eagle's skin into a hard shell and sent him to live in the ocean. Glooscap said to Big Eagle, "From now on you will be known as Turtle. Your shell will protect you from your enemies. Whenever danger threatens, just crawl into your shell."

Then Glooscap turned Cornflower into a turtle as well and the couple lived in the ocean for many happy years. Some say they are still there!

And now you know how turtles originated.

Origin of Wild Rice

An Ojibway Legend

The Ojibway Indians of the Great Lakes region in North America have harvested wild rice for many generations. Wild rice grows in lakes on stalks that stick out of the water and look something like cornstalks. When it is harvest time for wild rice, gatherers go out into the lake in their canoes, and gather the rice using two tapered sticks. Then they take home the wild rice and dry the rice in the sun. When the rice is dry, it can be cooked and eaten.

How did the Ojibway Indians learn about wild rice? Well, here is the legend.

L<small>IL'</small> R<small>ABBIT</small> was a young boy who lived with his grandmother — so the story goes. As Lil' Rabbit grew older, his grandmother expected him to help find food for the household. Each day Lil' Rabbit went into the deep woods to see what he could find for the next meal. He always took his bow and arrows and hunting knife with him in case he saw something to bring home for their evening meal.

One day Lil' Rabbit was completely unsuccessful. He did not see a single thing that even resembled supper. He was afraid to go home empty-handed because his grandmother might scold him for being a poor hunter.

After traveling on for some time, Lil' Rabbit still could find anything to bring home for supper. At last he came to a lake where heads of wild rice stalks were sticking out of the water. At that time, he did not know that wild rice could be eaten, but he decided to gather some of it anyway. He quickly made a canoe from the bark of a large birch tree, gathered up many of the wild rice stalks, and threw them into his canoe to take home. Certainly his grandmother would be able to see that he had *tried* to find something for supper.

As he continued his journey home, night came very suddenly. Lil' Rabbit thought he might lose his way in the dark so he decided to camp out and return home in the morning.

As he lay asleep Lil' Rabbit had a vision and heard one of the wild rice stalks he had gathered call out to him. "Lil' Rabbit, sometimes people eat seeds. They taste very good. First dry them, and then cook them."

Lil' Rabbit woke up from his sleep with a start. As he made his way home he remembered his vision and shared it with his grandmother. The two of them took the rice and dried it. Later they threshed the rice, cooked it, and ate it. The wild rice provided a very delicious meal.

Since that day, Ojibway Indians have gathered and eaten wild rice.

And now you know why they do.

Part Two:
How Stories

How Birds Can Be Teachers

A Pawnee Legend

GREY OWL was a member of the Pawnee Indian tribe. He loved being out of doors, and he loved going for walks. He was especially fond of watching the creatures of the earth find food and care for their young.

One day when Grey Owl was out walking in the prairie grass he came upon a bird's nest. The nest was hidden in some tall grasses, just about where he was going to place his next step. Grey Owl nearly stepped on the nest, but stopped in his tracks just in time.

The bird's nest was tucked inside a cluster of long grasses and had six oval-shaped eggs in it. Peering a little closer, Grey Owl heard a tiny sound coming from one of the eggs. He watched as a baby bird popped out of the egg, closely followed by five more baby birds from other eggs. Soon there were six babies in the nest and Grey Owl stood in wonder, having watched them hatch.

As the hatching of the baby birds was happening, the parents of the new baby birds were flying above the nest, watching Grey Owl. Even though the parent birds had food in their mouths, ready to feed their babies as soon as they hatched, they were also prepared to protect their babies from danger. The parents were anxiously flying around making threatening noises, warning Grey Owl not to do harm to their children.

Grey Owl smiled at the anxious parents, and nodded to them, to say that he would not harm their children. As he walked slowly back to his village he thought about what he had seen and how different parents were in his village.

Village parents did not always look after their children as carefully as the birds looked after their children. Sometimes human parents were thoughtless or careless about their children's needs. Grey Owl gave a lot of thought to these things as he walked home.

Some days later, Grey Owl went back to the bird's nest to see what was happening. He saw that the baby birds had grown and were stretching their wings, ready to fly. Their parents were kept very busy feeding the fledglings that would soon leave their nest.

"This is an amazing scene," Grey Owl said to himself. "If only my people would learn from the birds and treat their young the way the birds do. Then our homes would be happier and there would be a good future for our children. Our tribe would be strong and prosperous."

As the years passed by, Grey Owl became a spiritual leader of his tribe. The people saw that he had a great appreciation for nature and creatures of the earth. Grey Owl tried to put the teachings of the birds into practice.

And now you know how birds can be good teachers.

How Loon Became a Seabird

A Mi'kmaq Legend

BELIEVE IT OR NOT, Loon used to be a creature of the land. Loon was unable to swim, although he wished he could. He admired birds that made their homes in the water, like ducks, geese, and swans. He longed to be able to dive and swim.

Our story begins this way. Because he used to live on the land, Loon chose to live with the Mi'kmaq people in their village.

The people were not pleased with the arrangement and regarded Loon as a real nuisance. Loon was always getting into things and generally bothering people. He wandered in and out of their wigwams without being invited and was constantly getting under foot. A Mi'kmaq woman might be picking up a bedroll and Loon would be under it. When a family sat down to enjoy dinner, Loon would show up to eat. He was really quite an annoying bird.

Perhaps Loon was bored and that is why he bothered people so much. Loon did like to look over the ocean and admire the ducks and geese and swans that were quite at home in the ocean. Of course he could not join them because he could not swim. This did not stop him from wishing he could.

One day Glooscap happened to be in the village and was cooking a pot of fresh beans. When Loon smelled the beans he made his way over to where Glooscap was cooking. Immediately Loon began eating the tasty beans.

"Leave my food alone," Glooscap warned Loon, but Loon went right on eating.

"If you don't stop eating my food," Glooscap said, "I will throw you into the sea." This was just what Loon wanted. He knew that if Glooscap said something, he meant it. This could be Loon's lucky day!

"Please don't do that," Loon pleaded. "Don't throw me in the water. Throw me in the fire, but not in the water, please."

Glooscap ignored Loon's pleadings. He grabbed Loon by his wings and threw him into his canoe. Loon tried to look frightened, but this is just what he wanted. Glooscap paddled far away from shore and threw Loon into the open sea.

"There," Glooscap said, "let's see how much you enjoy your new home. This is where you will live from now on."

Quickly, Glooscap paddled his canoe back to shore.

In the meantime, Loon could not have been happier. "Just what I wanted, Just what I wanted," he kept saying to himself.

And ever since then loons have lived in the water — and enjoyed it.

And now you know how Loon got to be a creature of the sea.

How to Call Moose
A Wabanaki Legend

A LONG TIME AGO, Moose was so tall that he was able to eat leaves off the tops of trees. Unfortunately, he was so tall that he could hardly reach the ground to eat grass — and he liked to eat grass. When Moose walked around, there was a real danger that he would step on other creatures because he could not see them.

It happened that the Creator looked down one day and saw that life was not easy for Moose. He felt sorry for Moose because he was so large. The Creator also realized that people were in danger of accidentally being trampled on by Moose. The Creator called on Glooscap, His spiritual helper, to assist Him in solving Moose's problem. Glooscap called all the people and animals to a council and announced that Moose was in for a change. He was too tall for his own good. Moose did not hear Glooscap's call so he was not at the council.

Glooscap decided to invite Moose to the council meeting. He asked for a strip of birch-bark, just large enough to make a megaphone. He rolled the birch-bark into a funnel-shaped horn with a small end to blow into, and a large end where sound would come out. The first time he called Moose, people could only hear a faint sound and Moose did not appear. Glooscap called two more times, and though the sound got louder, Moose still did not come.

On the fourth try Glooscap called louder than ever. This time Moose heard Glooscap's call and quickly came to the council meeting.

"I have a surprise for you," Glooscap said to Moose. "I am going to make you shorter so you do not have to eat leaves off tree tops. Also when you are smaller you will not have to be afraid of stepping on people and little animals. Now, come to me." Moose walked over to Glooscap.

Glooscap grasped Moose's head by the horns and bent his head down until he was the desired size. Moose seemed quite pleased. Then Glooscap announced, "From this day on, this is the size you will be."

From that day on Moose has been the size he is today, and whenever a hunter wants to call Moose, he makes a horn out of birch-bark and blows into it.

And now you know why Moose is not too tall.

You also know how to call Moose.

How Yellow Mouse Fooled Owl
A Creek Legend

Owl is a very vain bird and she likes to think that everyone is afraid of her. Sometimes Owl hoots as loudly as she can just to frighten other creatures. At night she sometimes sleeps in a deep, dark cave so she can be as mysterious as possible. This story will show what happened to Owl because she was too puffed up with pride.

ONE AFTERNOON, when Owl was trying to have a nap, she found she could not sleep. It was simply too hot in her dusty cave. She decided to leave her cave to see if anyone else was awake. That way she could bother them. When she found no one outside her cave Owl said to herself, "Aha! Everyone has hidden from me. They are all afraid of me."

Owl looked around some more and then saw several tiny yellow mice sitting near a large gray rock. Quickly she flew over to where they were. As soon as the yellow mice spied Owl, they all ran away to hide. "An owl! An owl!" they all shrieked, as they ran for cover.

Owl liked what she saw. The mice were indeed afraid of her. She settled down near a mouse hole and called out. "You there, Mouse. Are you in this hole?"

"Yes, I am," replied a little yellow mouse, "and I am not coming out."

"But why not?" asked Owl. "I want to ask you something. Tell me; what do the creatures that live around here call me?"

"They call you Night Chieftain," said the little yellow mouse.

Owl liked what she was hearing and asked the little mouse to repeat what she had said. The little yellow mouse repeated, "Creatures around here call you Night Chieftain."

"Come closer and whisper into my ear," said Owl,

hoping to lure the little mouse out of the den. The little yellow mouse would have none of it and called out, "You are a miserable, vain, conceited, old wicked bird." With that the little mouse vanished deep inside her hole.

By this time Owl was raging with anger. "Just wait till I catch you, Mouse," she warned. "I'll teach you a lesson. I am not ever leaving this hole until you come out, even if I have to stay here forever."

Owl did not know that the little yellow mouse had slipped through an underground passageway and joined her friends. This was a successful way to escape Owl. The little yellow mouse told her friends what had happened.

In the meantime, Owl still waited outside the mouse hole for the little yellow mouse to come out. This did not happen, because the little mouse had safely joined her friends in the secret underground passageway that joined all the mouse holes.

Owl waited outside the mouse hole for one day, two days, three days, four days, and even longer. Finally, she died of hunger and thirst — a victim of her own puffed up pride.

And now you know how Owl learned a lesson: pride goes before a fall.

How Porcupine Got Quills
A Chippewa Legend

EVERYONE KNOWS that Porcupines have sharp quills on their backs and on their tails. When animals were first created, however, Porcupines did not have quills.

It happened that one day when big Brown Bear was looking for food and he spied Porcupine and decided to eat him. Porcupine quickly scampered up a tall tree so Brown Bear could not reach him. For a long time Porcupine was afraid to come down from the tree because Brown Bear might be waiting for him. Finally, Porcupine got so hungry that he simply had to come down from the tree. He was getting very weak and he needed to eat some food.

Porcupine began to search for something to eat, so he looked under a thorn bush for some bugs. Suddenly he noticed that the thorns of the thorn bush were very sharp. They pricked him. Porcupine suddenly had a brilliant idea. He broke off a few branches of the thorn bush and put them on his back. The next time Brown Bear tried to catch Porcupine, Porcupine simply rolled himself into a ball and lay still. When Brown Bear tried to touch him, sharp thorns on Porcupine's back pricked him. Brown Bear had to go away without hurting Porcupine.

Nanabush, the trickster, saw what happened and called Porcupine over to him. "How did you learn that trick?" he asked Porcupine. "Who taught you to put prickly branches of the thorn bush on your back?"

Porcupine answered, "I am always in danger when Brown Bear comes along so I put thorn bush branches on my back to protect myself. It was my own idea. The thorns pricked Brown Bear and kept him away from me."

Nanabush took some clay and put it on Porcupine's back. Then he took branches from a thorn bush and peeled them until they were white.

He stuck the branches in the clay on Porcupine's back. "There," Nanabush said, "now you will always have thorns to protect you. We will call them quills."

The next day Wolf came along and pounced on Porcupine, but the thorns on Porcupine's back pricked him. Wolf ran away howling.

Brown Bear stayed away from Porcupine too. He knew that Porcupine had protection.

And now you know how Porcupine got his quills.

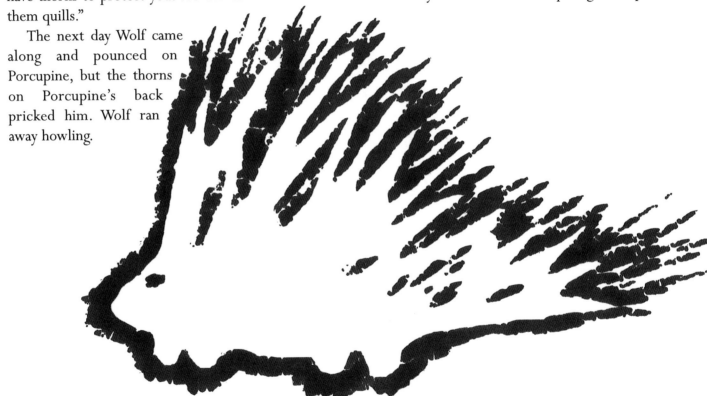

How Spotted Eagle Earned His Feather

A Mohawk Legend

It used to be the custom in many Native American Indian tribes that when a young man did something brave he would be awarded an eagle feather. Spotted Eagle was a young Mohawk Indian boy who wanted to earn an eagle feather, but he did not know what he could do to earn it.

At that time everything was going well in the Mohawk village where Spotted Eagle lived. The weather was pleasant, the river was brimming with fish, and there was a wealth of food for everyone to eat.

One day, without warning, things changed. For an extended length of time, no rains fell, creeks and rivers dried up, and game became scarce. Each day the village hunters went out to find game, and each day they came back with nothing.

Spotted Eagle respected and lived with his family, but he began to worry that things were not good for his people. He wondered if there was anything he could do to help out and perhaps earn his feather.

One day a hunter came back into the village looking as though he had been beaten up. As the women of the village bathed his battered wounds the hunter poured out his story.

"After hunting for hours, I finally found a deer to shoot," he explained. "As I shot my arrow at the deer, a pack of ferocious wolves attacked me and ran off with the deer. Now I have no food to bring to the village." Then the hunter closed his eyes and slept for a long time.

When the chief of the tribe heard about the hunter's experience, he called a council. During the discussion, it was decided that the ferocious wolves should be hunted down. "If we do not do that," the chief announced, "the wolves will take our food source from us!"

The village hunters got organized to go into the forest to search for the dangerous wolves. They decided to travel in small groups of two or three. It was agreed that if someone in one of the groups spotted the wolves, a hunter from the group would inform the larger group and collectively the hunters would go after the wolves. Although he was quite young, Spotted Eagle was selected to go with his father, and Spotted Eagle was very excited about it. Perhaps now he could do something brave and earn his eagle feather.

The eager hunters went off into the woods to pursue the wolf pack. Then, sure enough, after a brief search, Spotted Eagle and his father spied the wolf pack. Spotted Eagle's father asked Spotted Eagle to stand watch over the wolf pack while he went to search for the rest of the hunters.

The wolves seemed content as Spotted Eagle watched them. They were resting. Night began falling when the wolf pack started to move out. They had spotted a deer and the pack decided to pursue it. Spotted Eagle cautiously followed the wolf pack, well aware that they might get too far away and the hunters might not be able to find him. Then Spotted Eagle had an idea.

"Maybe if I shoot the lead wolf," he said to himself, "the pack will stay in one place and decide what to do. They will not have a leader to guide them before the hunters arrive."

Spotted Eagle watched carefully and as the wolf pack began to circle the deer, he identified the leader of the pack. The lead wolf was a big, dangerous-looking white wolf. Bravely, Spotted Eagle carefully drew his bow, aimed an arrow, and fired. His arrow struck the giant white wolf in the side and he let out a loud yelp. Then the wolf turned his gaze toward Spotted Eagle and quickly began running directly toward Spotted Eagle. Spotted Eagle aimed again and let a second arrow fly. Although his arrow struck the target, the great wolf kept coming toward the young hunter.

Quickly Spotted Eagle drew his knife and as the great wolf sprang towards him, he plunged the knife into the wolf's stomach. Without another sound, the white leader wolf fell dead at Spotted Eagle's feet. When the other wolves saw that their leader was dead, they all ran away. Spotted Eagle stood his ground in a complete daze. He could not believe what he had done.

When Spotted Eagle's father and the other hunters finally reached Spotted Eagle, they were amazed at his bravery and skill. No one in the tribe had ever killed such a great wolf before. There was no doubt about it, Spotted Eagle had earned his feather.

As soon as the hunters returned to the village, Spotted Eagle was honored with a big feast. At the feast he was awarded an eagle feather.

And you know how Spotted Eagle earned his feather.

How Whale Kept His Promise
A Haida Legend

Although it rains a great deal on the Canadian West Coast, the rain does not aggravate the Indians who live in that area. They appreciate the rain. According to local legend, it did not always rain that much on the West Coast. The heavy rains came after a young whale was stranded in an inlet off the West Coast beach many years ago.

LONG AGO, when an unusually high tide occurred, a young sperm whale swam into a shallow inlet and began to bask in the warmth of the sun. He soon fell asleep and slept on for several hours.

When he finally woke up, he discovered that the tide had gone out and he was stuck in the shallow water of the inlet. Taken by surprise, the young whale thrashed about in the shallow water, but was unable to cross the bridge of sand that prevented him from reaching the ocean.

Several days went by, nothing changed, and the young whale became desperate. He was afraid that the water in the inlet would dry up and he would die.

After a few more days passed, some Indians arrived in the inlet in their dugout boats and saw the trapped whale. "Please don't leave me here," Whale called out the Indians. "I will not hurt you; in fact, I cannot even swim anymore because the water is too shallow." After they overcame their fear, the Indians paddled over to Whale.

"How did you get here?" one of the Indians asked Whale. Whale explained that an unusually high tide had washed him into the inlet and gone out when he was sleeping. He could not get across the sand bridge that the tide left behind. Whale also said that he was very hungry and asked for food. His new acquaintances felt sorry for Whale and some of them caught some fish and gave them to Whale.

They kept up this arrangement for several weeks and gradually became good friends with Whale. Friends, of course, share experiences, and so the Indians told Whale about the dry spell. They also mentioned that many forest fires had occurred that summer. The weather simply got hotter and hotter each day.

"Perhaps I can help," said Whale. "If you can help me get back into the ocean, I will swim north and ask the Great Spirit to send rain." The Indians were skeptical about Whale's offer but decided to keep providing him with food. They also offered prayers on his behalf.

Several weeks went by, and eventually a very high tide came in and filled the inlet with plenty of water. Now Whale was able to swim back to the ocean. As he swam out of the inlet, and just before he dove into the depths of the ocean, he called out, "Thank you for supplying me with food and taking care of me so well. I have not forgotten my promise. I will speak to the Great Spirit."

Whale returned safely to the ocean, but the forest fires in the area grew more intense and the weather got even hotter. The Indians fought the fires with everything they had, and just when they were about to give up hope, a few raindrops began to fall. Then a strange light came over the horizon and raindrops began to fall faster and faster. Soon the heavens opened up and heavy rains poured over the forests. Quickly the fires went out and the delighted Indians held a ceremony and thanked the Great Spirit for helping them. Then they realized that they ought to thank Whale as well. After all, he had kept his promise.

From that day to this, the Indians of the Canadian North West Coast are very grateful whenever it starts to rain. They remember Whale's promise.

And you know how the First Nations of the Canadian West Coast came to appreciate rain.

Part Three:
Why Stories

Why Badger is Humble

An Interior Salish Legend

A LONG TIME AGO, Coyote – the trickster – and Fox lived in the same lodge. One day they were very hungry but could not find anything to eat. They decided to go hunting, but after a fruitless search for game, they returned to their lodge empty-handed.

Fox then decided to leave the country and live elsewhere. He thought that hunting for game might be better in another place. Coyote disagreed with Fox. Fox moved away, but Coyote stayed in their lodge.

Coyote lost his hunting partner when Fox moved away, and now all Coyote could find to eat were insects and leaves. One day, Coyote learned that there was food in a nearby village, but he also knew that the villagers would not want to share their food with the trickster. They knew him too well. The only way he was going to get food was by fooling the villagers. Of course Coyote was good at that. He loved playing tricks and fooling people, so he began to scheme.

It happened that Badger lived in the village that Coyote was going to trick into giving him food. Badger was a handsome fellow, a proud warrior, and a good hunter. Everyone in the village admired and respected him. All the fathers hoped that Badger would choose one of their daughters as his wife, but Badger had other ideas. He wanted to marry a woman from another village.

One day, Badger's four sisters went to the river to bathe. They saw a beautiful woman at the river and invited her to visit the lodge where they lived with their brother Badger.

The woman was really Coyote in disguise. Badger liked the pretty woman. He did not realize the woman was really Coyote. Immediately Badger asked the attractive woman to marry him. She agreed, but asked if she could first take some food to her parents.

The beautiful woman then invited Badger's sisters to accompany her and bring a lot of food with them. Badger thought it was a nice plan, so the four sisters and the fine-looking woman went to Coyote's lodge with the food. The four sisters did not know it was Coyote's lodge. Badger's new friend asked Badger's sisters to remain outside the lodge while she went in with the food. In a few minutes, out stepped Coyote who was no longer disguised as the pretty woman. He laughed heartily at the sisters who had accompanied him with the food.

"Thank you for the food," Coyote gloated. "Now I will have enough to eat for many moons."

When the four sisters returned home and told Badger what had happened, he went straight to Coyote's lodge and chased him out of the country. Badger and his sisters tried to keep Coyote's trick a secret, but somehow the people in the village found out about it and made fun of Badger. Someone even said, "Poor Badger. He wanted to find a wife from somewhere else but he settled for Coyote."

Badger felt so badly that he scarcely showed himself around the village after that. The experience humbled him, and to this day all badgers are shy and humble.

And now you know why badgers are humble.

Why Beaver is Respected

A Dene Legend

There were once two mean cranky old uncles who lived in the Canadian north in Dene country. They worked hard to provide for their families, but they had a nephew who was very lazy. He refused to go hunting or do any useful task. Everyone in the village called him Slow Stone because he never did any chores around the village.

One day the two uncles decided to take Slow Stone hunting for beaver pelts. They went looking for a beaver lodge, and when they finally found a beaver lodge, the uncles cut a hole in the top of it. Then they lowered Slow Stone down into the beaver lodge, and told him to let them know if he saw any beavers coming to the surface. Then they waited for beavers to appear.

After the uncles had waited for several hours and no beaver came to the surface, they looked down inside the beaver lodge and saw Slow Stone fast asleep.

"Such a nephew is not worth having," they said to one another. Then they put the top back on the beaver lodge and left Slow Stone to the beavers. There was no way he could get out of the beaver lodge.

Soon the two beavers that lived in the lodge arrived home and found Slow Stone inside. "This poor man looks lost," they said to one another. "Let's give him some food and find out how he got here."

The two beavers started a fire and cooked some meat for Slow Stone. Then they began to talk with him and he told them his story.

"You mean your own two uncles left you trapped inside our lodge?" the beavers asked incredulously. "Why would anyone do that to a member of his own family?"

After supper the kind beavers cut a fresh hole in the roof of their lodge and helped Slow Stone climb out of the lodge. As he left he told them that he would never go hunting for beavers.

When Slow Stone arrived in his village, everyone was surprised to see him, especially the two mean uncles. They had told the villagers that Slow Stone was dead.

After his adventure, Slow Stone never hunted beavers, but he never told anyone why.

But now you know why beavers are respected.

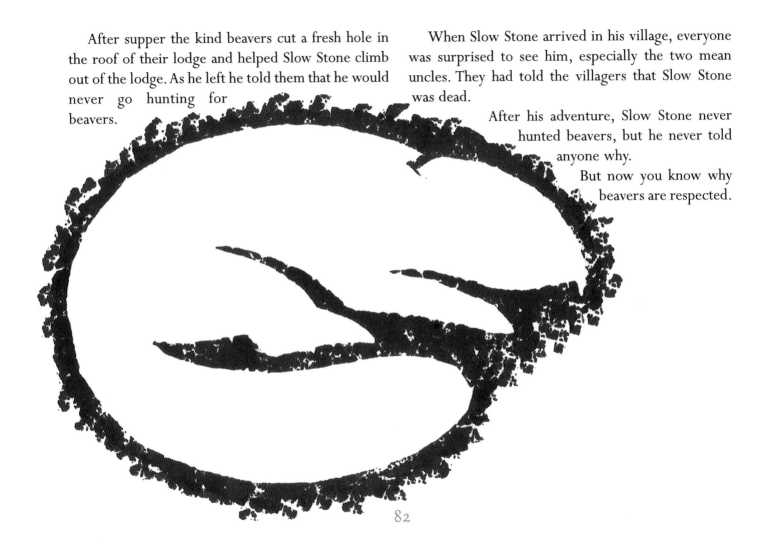

Why Buzzards Are Bald
An Algonquian Legend

One day Iktûmni, the trickster, was making his way home after spending an unsuccessful day looking for food. He was tired and hungry and not in a particularly good mood. Like people, the trickster sometimes tended to be unhappy when he was unsuccessful in performing a task.

Suddenly, Buzzard appeared before Iktûmni. He seemed to have come out of nowhere, but Iktûmni, crafty fellow that he was, decided immediately to take advantage of the situation.

"Why don't you give me a ride home?" the trickster asked Buzzard. "You have such large wings and a big back, and I am so tired. I would really appreciate a ride home."

Although Buzzard knew all about Iktûmni's reputation for fooling people and playing tricks on them, he agreed to take the trickster home. Unknown to Iktûmni, Buzzard also had a tricky plan in mind. Buzzard took off with Iktûmni on his back, but they had not gone far when Buzzard started to fly in a circle. Iktûmni noticed this and cried out, "Why are we circling? You know where my home is. Take me there. This is an order!"

Suddenly a large hollow tree came into view below the pair and Buzzard quickly dipped his wings and dumped Iktûmni into the hollow tree. There was no way Iktûmni could get out. He was stuck! He cried for help, but there was no one to hear him. Buzzard flew away laughing.

Eventually, several woman walked by the hollow tree in which the trickster had been dumped and Iktûmni heard them talking. Fortunately, Iktûmni had a few raccoon skins with him and he shoved parts of them through a crack in the dead tree for the women to see. He knew they would want the raccoon skins.

Taking turns with an axe they had with them, the women chopped a hole in the tree trunk large enough to reach the raccoon skins. When they finished cutting the hole, they saw the trickster's face inside. Quickly the frightened women dropped the axe and ran away.

Now able to free himself, Iktûmni climbed out of the tree trunk and threw himself on the ground, pretending to be dead. Then he waited for birds of prey to come and devour him — magpies, hawks, and eagles — all came and began pecking at him. Iktûmni took the abuse, waiting patiently for Buzzard to come and join in.

When Buzzard finally showed up, Iktûmni rose quickly and tore the feathers off of Buzzard's scalp. Now Buzzard's head feathers were gone and he was suddenly bald. He has remained so to this day!

And now you know why Buzzards are bald.

Why Coyote Looks at His Stomach:

An Okanagan Legend

WHEN THE WORLD was first created, animals did not have names. It was sometimes hard to call the animals to council because they did not have names.

One day the Creator sent word that all animals should meet together. He then announced that they should have individual names so he could call their individual names when it was time for council. "Come to my lodge tomorrow," he said, "and you can all choose names for yourselves."

Coyote, the trickster listened to what the Creator had to say and started to think. Even though everyone knew who Coyote was, he was thinking of getting a new name.

"Maybe I will take the name Grizzly Bear," he said, "that way everyone will know that I am strong and fierce. Maybe I will pick the name Eagle and fly higher than anyone else."

He did not know that among other creatures he already had a nickname – the Imitator. The other animals secretly called him the Imitator because he always copied everything others were doing.

Coyote's wife suggested that he should keep his name since it suited him. Mrs. Coyote worried about her husband. He was so restless and never seemed to be satisfied with things.

"I want a more powerful name," Coyote said, and with those words he went to bed. He wanted to get a good night's sleep so he could wake up early and be first in line to choose a new name for himself.

The next morning, before the sun was up, Coyote arrived at the Creator's lodge and asked for the name Eagle.

"That name has been taken," said the Creator.

"Then give me the name Grizzly Bear," said Coyote.

"That name has been taken too," said the Creator.

Coyote then asked for the name Salmon and the name Wolf Hound, and was informed that they too were already taken. The Creator asked Coyote to look inside himself and see what name would suit him. The Creator wanted to give Coyote the power to do useful things, or to do harm. It would be up to Coyote to choose his actions.

When the Creator asked Coyote to look inside himself, Coyote thought the Creator wanted him to look at his stomach, but the Creator meant he should look at his heart. Because Coyote did not listen correctly, this is why even today he spends so much time looking at his stomach.

And now you know why Coyote looks at his stomach.

Why Coyote's Eyes are Red
A Shuswap Legend

WOLVERINE WAS SOMETIMES in the habit of amusing himself by taking his eyeballs out, throwing them in the air, and catching them. Animals who watched him do this wondered how he could perform such a trick. Wolverine only laughed, and told no one his secret.

One day Coyote, the trickster, saw Wolverine playing his strange game and thought he would try it himself. Taking his eyeballs out, he threw them into the air, but they would not land in his eyes when they came down. He tried again, but his eyeballs simply would not fall back into their orbits.

Coyote kept trying, but he was not very successful. He discovered that even when his eyeballs *did* fall into their sockets, they would not stay there. Coyote was getting frustrated.

As Coyote was experimenting with Wolverine's game, he did not notice Magpie walk up behind him, grab his eyeballs and make off with them. Now Coyote was completely blind.

"What a fool I was," Coyote said to himself. I was trying to do a trick I knew nothing about. If I could only find some bearberries I could make eyeballs out of them."

Coyote crawled around on the ground, hoping to find some bearberries. He felt all around him, hoping that one of the bushes he touched had bearberries on it. Finally, he put his hand on a rosebush, and taking two rose berries, he put them into his orbits. Now he could see, only not as well as before. Besides, the rose berries were larger and slightly red in color. From that day to this, Coyote has had large reddish eyes.

And now you know why.

Why Dogs Bark
A Kiowa Legend

It may be a bit hard to believe, but dogs used to talk to human beings. One day they lost their ability to talk, and here is the story.

One day Saynday, the trickster, was on his way to the village where the dogs lived. He had a special message for the dogs and wanted to have a council with them. He wanted to tell them something important.

As Saynday entered the village he was startled by all the noise.

"Hush, everybody," Saynday ordered. "I have something important to say to you. I need to speak with you."

"Of course you need to speak," said one of the dogs. "We all do."

"Yes," said another dog, "Everyone has something to say. Why should we listen to you?"

Then all the dogs chorused, "Saynday has something to say, and so do we all." Then they went right on talking and kept getting louder and louder. Saynday was getting very upset.

"If you don't stop talking," Saynday commanded, "something very bad is going to happen to you. I am not going to warn you again."

Ignoring Saynday, the dogs kept right on talking.

Saynday called on his magic powers and spoke angrily to the dogs. "I have warned you but you would not listen. From now on, none of you is ever going to be able to speak. You will be able to growl and bark and yap, but you will never be able to talk again. When you bark, no human being will be able to understand you. From this day on you will only be able to talk to people with your bark and by wagging your tails."

That is the way it has been ever since. Dogs cannot speak, only bark.

And now you know why.

Why Eagle Went Hungry

A Sioux Legend

Eagle has often been called king of the birds and it is said that he rules the skies. Eagle can fly higher than any other bird and other birds and animals fear and respect him. Sometimes, however, Eagle's status as king of the birds makes him a little bit too proud. This story will show what happened.

ONE DAY, when Beaver Woman was chopping wood near the river, she suddenly heard a swooping noise in the sky. It was Eagle, who flapped his mighty wings and swiftly perched himself on the top of a tree just above Beaver Woman. Beavers always dive under water when they hear unexpected noises, and Beaver Woman did just that.

Eagle wanted to speak with Beaver Woman so he decided to wait until she emerged from the river. He stared impatiently at the water, waiting for Beaver Woman to reappear. After a long wait Beaver Woman came to the surface of the water. She saw Eagle perched on the tree, waiting for her arrival.

"What right have you to disturb a hard-working woman?" she asked Eagle. "Why did you rush over here so quickly?"

"Well," said Eagle. "I happen to be hungry. Do you have anything for me to eat?"

"No," said Beaver Woman. "Why don't you do as everyone else does and work for your food?"

"That is all very well for you to say," remarked Eagle, "but I am king of the birds. I do not cut down trees and eat bark and weeds and live in a mud-plastered wigwam. I am a warrior, not an old woman. Now get me something to eat."

"It is too bad that there are selfish creatures such as yourself," Beaver Woman commented. "I see no reason why you do not work like the rest of us do.

I love my work, taking care of my family and providing for them. You would do well to follow my example. It would be a better world if you did." Then Beaver Woman dove back into the water.

Eagle waited a long, long time for Beaver Woman to reappear, but she never did. Finally, Eagle flew away, still hungry. Sometimes Eagle is still very hungry, but he does not expect others to get his food for him.

And you know why Eagle needed to learn a lesson.

Why Eagles Are Respected
An Iroquois Legend

NANABOZHO, the trickster, could be a very successful hunter if he was in the mood, and all the animals knew this. The trickster knew how to cast magic spells that brought creatures close to him so he could shoot them with his bow and arrows. The trickster also had the ability to play tricks on people and animals and he often did this.

Sometimes Nanabozho would call eagles to himself saying there was fresh meat for them to eat on the ground below them. When hungry eagles listened to Nanabozho and flew down from the sky to eat the meat, the trickster would shoot them and take their feathers. Then the trickster would trade the feathers for other items he wanted – like food.

One day Nanabozho made a big mistake. He called the eagles to tell them there was meat for them on the ground when suddenly the gigantic Mother of Eagles swooped down on him. She had heard about the tricks Nanabozho played on eagles and she wanted to put a stop to it. When the trickster saw Mother of Eagles he hid inside a hollow log, but Mother of Eagles picked up the log in her claws and flew high into the sky with it. As she soared into the sky she spied a large eagle's nest perched on the top of a very tall tree without branches. The nest was empty because the baby eagles that had lived in it had grown up and flown away. Quickly Mother of Eagles dropped the log into the nest.

When Nanabozho landed in the eagle's nest he knew he was in trouble. The nest was located on the top of such a tall tree, high above the ground. With no branches on the tree, the trickster would not be able to climb down. The Nanabozho was very fortunate, however, because he had his medicine bag with him. In the bag was a little dried meat so at least he had something to eat. He did not know how long

Mother of Eagles was going to keep him captive in the nest. As the days passed, the trickster grew worried. There was no way he could get to the ground from his high perch atop the tall tree.

After several days, Mother of Eagles flew back to the nest where she had left Nanabozho. She wanted to make an agreement with the trickster. "I will release you to the ground" she said, "but you must promise never to trick or harm another eagle. From now on you must respect eagles and not play tricks on them."

Of course the trickster agreed. What else could he do? Then Mother of Eagles swooped down, picked up Nanabozho in her claws, and dropped him on the ground. Solemnly, the trickster promised never again to tease, trick, hunt, or shoot eagles. And he never did.

And now you know why Eagles are respected.

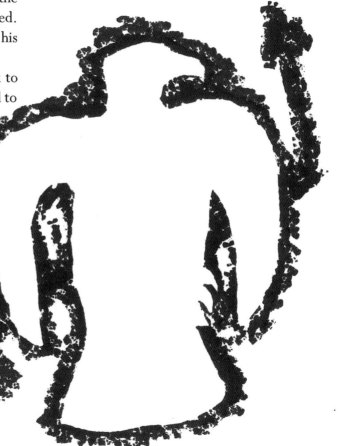

Why Fawn Has Spots

A Dakota Legend

When the Creator made animals, He gave each of them a special gift by which to protect themselves from their enemies.

He gave Porcupine quills.

He gave Skunk a very strong smell.

He gave Buffalo horns.

He gave Wolf strong teeth.

He gave Panther speed.

He gave Rabbit two colors: white for winter and brown for summer.

He gave Bear sharp claws.

He gave Mole special digging skills.

Almost every creature had a very special gift to help him hide from or escape from his enemies.

One day the Creator looked down and saw Mother Deer with her baby, Fawn. Wolf was chasing them, and because Fawn could not keep up to Mother Deer, Mother Deer ordered Fawn to hide in some bushes. Naturally, after a long search Wolf found Fawn, but Mother Deer quickly turned back and fought off Wolf's attack.

Mother Deer prayed to the Creator and thanked Him for the speed He had given her to outrun Wolf. Then she asked the Creator why He had not done something special for Fawn. She asked if Fawn could also have the gift of speed and be able to outrun Wolf, or perhaps Fawn could have some other special gift of protection.

The Creator felt sorry for Mother Deer because of the danger that befell Fawn and decided to do something about it. He took a paintbrush and carefully painted spots on Fawn until he blended in with the shadows in the grass.

From then on, Fawn could easily hide in the bush and elude his enemies. He was given a special gift of protection given by the Creator.

And you know why Fawn has spots.

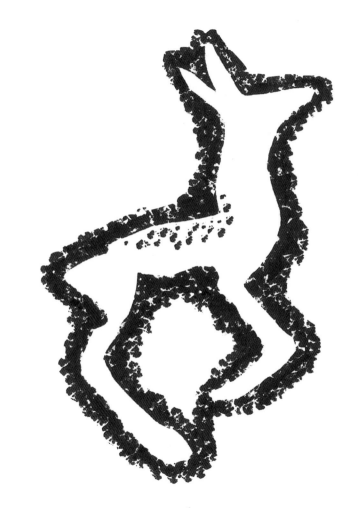

Why Moose Has Loose Skin

A Swampy Cree Legend

MANY MOONS AGO, when the world first began, two things were different about animals. First, all animals were the same gray color and second, they were all friendly with one another. Otter was a friend to Squirrel, Squirrel was a friend to Wolf, and Wolf was a friend to Moose.

Life was going well, until one winter when the world was fiercely cold. The animals suffered in the harsh, blasting winds, ice-covered trees and bushes, and huge drifts of snow. Even deep caves did not provide enough warmth for the animals. The earth was completely covered with a thick blanket of snow and food was scarce. Everyone was relieved when spring finally came.

Brown Bear called a council of the animals and spoke to his friends. "We have all endured a terrible winter and we hope there is never another like it. We have discovered that our fur coats are not warm enough for such a harsh winter. We must ask the Creator to give us warmer coats."

Everyone agreed with Brown Bear and immediately several animals began to offer additional suggestions.

Porcupine, who was quite vain, said, "While we are at it, let us ask the Creator for horns as well. Horns can be useful items. I think horns would be helpful for everyone."

After some discussion the animals agreed to contact Wisakedjak, the trickster, and discuss the matter with him. They thought Wisakedjak could contact the Creator with their request. Wisakedjak agreed to do so, and after speaking with the Creator, the trickster reported back to the animals.

"I am happy to announce that we can obtain thicker, warmer coats as a gift from the Creator," said the trickster. "What kind of coats would you like to have? There is a wide variety of coats to choose from including a variety of sizes and colors."

Wisakedjak set a date for the animals to visit a cave where coat samples would be made available. Everyone was very excited. Every animal wanted to obtain a warmer and different colored coat. In the meantime Wisakedjak went to the cave to get things ready. He worked hard making many different colored coats. He also made some horns available.

The day came when everything was ready, and animals arrived from near and far to select their coats. They came from the hills, the plains, near the sea, and northern regions. After examining the various coats, the animals picked out the ones they wanted. Fawn wanted a coat with pretty spots, and Lynx chose a handsome yellow coat with little tufts on the ears. Porcupine seemed to forget all about horns when he saw a coat with sharp quills on it. This was the one he wanted.

Moose was late for the event because he stopped to eat so many times along the way to the cave. He was a very large animal and was always hungry. When he finally got to the cave, the only coat that was left was a large loose, brown colored coat. Moose put on the coat, and found it to be quite warm, but it fit poorly. Still, it was the only coat left, and Moose wanted to keep warm in the winter. From that day to this, Moose has had to wear his loose coat.

And now you know why.

Why Porcupine is Respected
A Tsimshian Legend

In historical times, the Tsimshian Indian tribe of the Canadian West Coast always had many successful hunters. The hunters were so successful that the animals that had not yet been hunted got very worried. One day Grizzly Bear called a council of the large animals that sleep during the winter to decide what to do.

"Something has to be done," said Grizzly Bear. "Too many of us are being hunted down by Tsimshian hunters. Soon there won't be any of us left. We must do something about this." All the animals at the council began to speak at once.

Grizzly Bear tried to calm the meeting with these words. "I would like to make a suggestion. I think we should ask the Creator to give us a longer, colder winter so that no hunter may attack us in our dens. I would like it to be so cold that no hunter can even venture out in the winter time."

Wolf spoke up. "Before we do that, why not ask all the smaller animals to come to our meeting. Let us invite Porcupine, Beaver, Raccoon, Muskrat, and Mink, down to the smallest animal like Mouse and even the insects that crawl on the earth. Let us hear what each one has to say before we decide."

Everyone liked Wolf's idea, so the next day all the animals were invited to the council meeting. Everyone came to the meeting.

Grizzly Bear started the meeting and outlined his plan to ask the Creator for a very cold winter to stop Tsimshian hunters from hunting during the winter months.

Porcupine spoke up.

"Perhaps we ought to think of another plan," he said. "Many smaller animals do not have fur coats thick enough to withstand a much colder winter. What will happen to them?"

Grizzly Bear suggested that everyone ignore Porcupine. He felt that as long as the larger animals were taken care of, the plan was good enough.

Porcupine would not give up and spoke again. "If we ask for a very long, cold winter, that will leave a very short summer. How will plants be able to grow in a short summer? Trees, bushes and flowers will wither away and soon there will be no edible plants left on earth."

As Grizzly Bear listened to Porcupine he knew this was good advice.

"You have spoken wise words," Grizzly Bear said. "We do need the summer sunshine to grow plants." After the meeting, the animals asked the Creator for six months of winter and six months of summer. And it was so.

It happened that a few of the larger animals that sleep during the winter months did not like Porcupine's advice. They spread gossip about Porcupine among the other animals. Porcupine did not like to be insulted so he visited these animals and struck them with the quills on his tail. From that day to this, the other animals watch out for Porcupine.

And now you know why Porcupine is respected.

Why Possum is Shy
A Creek Legend

Believe it or not, Possum used to have a fine hairy tail, but today his tail is completely bare. Possum was very proud of his large and bushy tail and he was always proud to show it off. Some of the other animals got quite tired of his vanity.

One day Possum met Raccoon and discovered that Raccoon had a number of beautiful decorative bright circles on his tail. To Possum, they looked like rings of gold.

"What a fine tail you have," Possum said to Raccoon. At once Possum decided that he should have shiny rings on his tail too.

"You have a very fine tail too," Raccoon said to Possum, trying unsuccessfully to end the talk about his tail.

"I know I have a fine tail," said Possum, "but your tail has those beautiful rings on it. I would like to have some of those too. At least tell me how you got those attractive rings."

"Certainly," said Raccoon, feeling just a bit mischievous. "All you have to do is put some wooden rings of tree-bark on your tail, and then stick your tail into the embers of a glowing fire. The fire will permanently glue the rings to your tail. Be careful not to leave your tail in the fire too long because the hot embers might burn it."

Possum was very excited and ran off to do just what Raccoon had suggested. "Silly animal," Raccoon muttered to himself. "I sure hope he does not burn himself to death. He was just a bit too excited for my liking."

Possum had some difficulty getting the tree-bark rings on his tail, but after a while he managed to do so. He was sure the end result would be worth all the effort. Possum made a very warm fire and when he thought the embers were hot enough; he pushed his tail into the fire. Immediately, the heat of the fire gave him severe pain, but he was determined to endure it.

At last the embers burned down, and Possum crawled away to cool his tail and look at the result. When he finally looked back at his tail he saw that it was completely bare. All the hairs on it were burned off. In fact, he was lucky to have a tail at all. He began to cry, then changed his mind and decided to find Raccoon and punish him. As soon as Raccoon saw Possum coming, he ran away to hide. After searching for Raccoon for four days, Possum gave up on punishing him.

Today Possum lies low and does not show himself to very many creatures. He is so ashamed of his tail. He is also ashamed of how he fell for Raccoon's trick.
And now you know why Possum is shy.

Why Rabbit Turns White In Winter

A Cree Legend

As Wisakedjak, the trickster, was walking along one day he noticed that all the grass around him had turned brown and the leaves on the trees were gone. Fall had come early, so there was little for animals to eat and Wisakedjak felt sorry for them. He wondered if the Creator was angry at the animals or had He forgotten them. The trickster was also surprised that there was suddenly so little food for animals to eat.

Wisakedjak felt he had to do something about the situation. He decided to visit the animals and check on their food supply. He walked quite a distance into the forest, and when evening came, he stopped for the night. He built a makeshift teepee out of long tree branches and laid down in his teepee to sleep.

When Wisakedjak woke the next morning, he found the ground completely covered with snow. "This is a good thing," he said. "now I will be able to find all the animals by their tracks in the snow. Then I will be able to speak with them."

As the trickster walked along he could make out the tracks of Deer, Elk, Moose, Wolf, Fox, and Rabbit. He decided that he would visit each of them, and ask them about their food supply.

Even though Wisakedjak walked for a long distance, he was unable to find any of the animals. "I guess I must be lost," he said to himself. "Everything is covered in bright, white snow and I can hardly see where I am going. Perhaps I can find the river and then I will know where I am."

Suddenly, Wisakedjak spied a small, brown colored animal huddled under a small snow-covered bush right in front of him. "Hello, Brother Rabbit," the trickster called out, "I am lost and do not know where I am. I wonder if you could help me out. Can you tell me where the river is?"

Rabbit was glad to help. "Follow my tracks," he said. "I can lead you straight to the river."

Wisakedjak followed the tracks of the little brown rabbit and before long they had reached the river's edge. Wisakedjak was very grateful. Now he knew just where he was.

Wisakedjak spoke kindly to Rabbit. "I greatly appreciate your help, Brother Rabbit. Because you have been kind to me, I want to do something for you. I am going to change the color of your fur to white in the winter so your enemies will have a hard time finding you. In summertime you can be brown again."

Then, because Wisakedjak had the power to do so, he changed Brother Rabbit's fur to white.

From that day to this, Rabbit has been white in the winter and dark in the summer.

And now you know why.

Why Wolverine Has Short Legs
A Cree Legend

WISAKEDJAK, the trickster, knew a great deal about the animals of the forest because he spent much time with them. He knew all the secrets of the animals. He knew why Rabbit's tail is short, why Moose used to be extremely tall, why Beaver's tail is flat, and why Buzzard is bald.

Wisakedjak also knew that Wolverine had beautiful fur and very long legs and he liked to brag about these qualities. Whenever Wolverine ran a race with other animals, he always won because his legs were so long.

Wolverine was a very mischievous animal, and he liked to play tricks on other animals. Some of the tricks he played on other animals were quite mean.

One day some of the animals came to Wisakedjak and complained about Wolverine's tricks. The trickster tried to console the animals and had a long talk with Wolverine. Wolverine promised to be kinder, but the next day he was playing tricks on the other animals again.

A few days later Wolverine was walking past the trickster's teepee and as he passed, he looked inside. Wisakedjak was not at home so Wolverine crept in and took Wisakedjak's fire bag. Inside the bag were some dry sticks, some steel, and a piece of flint to make fire. Wolverine took the fire bag and hung it high on a long tree branch. Then he went off laughing, proud of the trick he had played on Wisakedjak.

When Wisakedjak came home that evening he was tired and hungry. He looked for his fire bag to start a fire and cook supper. The fire bag was nowhere to be found. As he continued to search, Wisakedjak noticed some tracks leading out of his teepee. He followed the tracks and soon came to a tall tree. When he looked up, he saw his fire bag, hanging from the highest branch.

Wisakedjak muttered angrily to himself as he climbed the tree to get his fire bag. "If I find out who did this, he will be punished," he promised. As the trickster reached the ground with his fire bag, he heard a scampering noise behind him. There was Wolverine, slyly watching Wisakedjak and laughing to himself. Wisakedjak called to Wolverine who came out of the bushes, looking not a bit sorry for what he had done.

Wisakedjak spoke to Wolverine. "You are always getting into mischief and I am going to punish you for playing mean tricks. From now on your legs will be very short and crooked and you will never be able to run fast again. As he spoke, Wolverine's long legs shrank. They have remained so to this very day.

So now you know why Wolverine has short legs.

Part Four:
Ten Tricky Trickster Tales

Copycat Coyote and Rattlesnake
A Sia Legend

Coyote, the trickster, and Rattlesnake were neighbors, but they did not know each other very well. They did not usually visit one another's lodges, but one day, things changed. Coyote had a plan, so he decided to make friends with Rattlesnake.

"Come to my lodge tonight," said Coyote to Rattlesnake. "Then we can have a warm supper and visit together. Perhaps we will get to know one another better."

Rattlesnake liked the idea, and agreed to go to Coyote's lodge. When he got to Coyote's lodge he discovered that Coyote was cooking some rabbit stew in a large pot on the stove.

Coyote did not particularly care for the noise of Rattlesnake's rattles as he moved along, but he pretended not to notice. Truthfully, Coyote was actually just a little bit afraid of Rattlesnake.

Coyote invited Rattlesnake to have some rabbit stew, but Rattlesnake politely refused.

"I am sorry, neighbor," he said. "I cannot eat your kind of food. I do not understand it."

"What kind of food do you eat?" Coyote wanted to know.

"I prefer the yellow flowers (pollen) of the corn plant," said Rattlesnake. Coyote hunted for some pollen and found it. He offered it to Rattlesnake.

"Put the pollen on my head," said Rattlesnake. "If you put it on the top of my head, I will eat it. I will be able to reach it with my very long tongue."

Coyote thought this was all a bit strange, but he did as Rattlesnake asked.

Soon Rattlesnake announced that he was going home and thanked Coyote for his hospitality. He invited Coyote to visit him the next day.

The following day as Coyote prepared to visit Rattlesnake's lodge, he decided to copy Rattlesnake. He wanted to make a noise like Rattlesnake, so he tied some pebbles to his tail to try to scare

Rattlesnake by making the pebbles rattle when he walked. Of course this did not work, but Rattlesnake told Coyote that he was just a little afraid of him because of the rattling noises Coyote was making.

Rattlesnake had a pot of tasty prairie dog meat cooking on his stove and invited Coyote to have supper with him. Prairie dog meat was one of Coyote's favorite foods, but he refused to eat any, saying, "I do not understand your food. Give me some pollen from a cornstalk and I will eat it. Put it on the top of my head so I can eat it."

Rattlesnake did not want to go near Coyote because he was pretending to be afraid of him. He cautiously went over to where the trickster was and put pollen on his head just as Coyote asked. Coyote soon found that he could not reach the pollen with his tongue because his tongue was not long enough. When he saw this, Rattlesnake began to laugh. Coyote was so embarrassed he soon left Rattlesnake's lodge shaking the pebbles on his tail as he went. Rattlesnake shouted, "O neighbor, I am so afraid of you!"

Coyote was so embarrassed that he left the country.

And you know why.

Coyote and Magpie Go Hunting
A Thompson Legend

One day Coyote, the trickster, accompanied Magpie on a hunting trip because he wanted to learn Magpie's hunting methods. Magpie was a very successful hunter and everyone admired him for it. Everyone knew that Magpie was especially good at hunting deer. This is how he worked.

Magpie carefully set a net snare close to his lodge and then went to the mountains to find a buck deer to lure into it. He drew the buck's attention by calling to it and then saying things like this.

"Hey there, you big clumsy buck," Magpie would call. "Did you know that you are very ugly? That is why no one wants to be friends with you. Why don't you go somewhere and live by yourself?"

Magpie's words made the big buck angry and he charged Magpie, who quickly took to his heels with the buck chasing him. The two kept running, but Magpie was always just a little ahead of the buck, ahead just enough to encourage him. When they reached the snare that Magpie had set up, Magpie jumped over it, but the buck did not. Magpie led the buck right into the snare where he was trapped. Magpie quickly killed the buck, and cut up the meat. Since the snare was very close to Magpie's lodge, he did not have to carry the meat very far. Soon he had roasted deer meat on his table.

When Coyote saw how Magpie had snared the buck he decided to imitate Magpie's method of hunting.

Coyote set up a snare very close to his lodge and went to the mountains to find a buck deer. He called the buck insulting names just as Magpie had done. The buck grew angry and began to chase Coyote. Coyote ran home as quickly as he could, and managed to stay ahead of the buck. When the two of them reached Coyote's snare, Coyote attempted to jump over it, but failed to do so. He fell right into his snare. So did the buck. The buck immediately began to attack Coyote.

The buck poked Coyote with his antlers and would have killed him if some of the village people had not helped Coyote out of the snow.

Coyote never again tried to use Magpie's hunting method.
And now you know why.

Coyote and Quail
A Pima Legend

ONE DAY, the Quail clan held a meeting to decide how to stop Coyote, the trickster, from playing tricks on them.

"One of the things I dislike most about Coyote is that he likes to chase us up a tree and keeps us there for a long time," said one of the clan members. "When he does this we cannot come down to eat or drink until he leaves."

"We must put a stop to this," said Chief Quail. We need four clan members who will volunteer to play a trick on Coyote. This trick will stop him from bothering us." Immediately four members agreed to undertake the task.

Chief Quail thanked the four members for volunteering. He announced that the trick would require sticks, feathers, and a thorny piece of cactus. The sticks and cactus were disguised to make a fake quail that would be covered with feathers. The sticks were made to look like the legs of the fake quail and the cactus was its body. The fake quail was pushed into a badger hole.

Now the plan was set. Sure enough, soon Coyote appeared, and the four volunteers went into hiding.

Coyote came along, his nose to the ground, sniffing for a quail. Suddenly the four hidden quails sang out, "Coyote is a foolish fellow." Coyote was shocked.

"How dare you quails make fun of me?" He said. "You little creatures have such nerve. Don't you know who I am? I can make your life miserable."

Coyote ran over to where the four quails were hiding but they scurried into the badger hole where the fake quail was hidden. Coyote reached into the badger hole and one by one brought out all four quails. He asked each one, "Were you the one making fun of me?" Each one in turn answered, "No."

Coyote reached into the badger hole one more time and brought out the fifth quail. This was the fake quail. "Were you the one making fun of me?" Coyote asked.

The fake quail gave no answer so Coyote dug his sharp teeth into what he thought was a real quail. Immediately he howled with pain from biting into the prickly cactus.

Coyote learned his lesson. He never chased quail again.

And now you know why.

Raven and the Magpies
A Tlinget Legend

RAVEN, THE TRICKSTER, was hungry so he took his nephews, the magpies, with him to fish for salmon. Magpies are kind of noisy birds, always chattering about something. At that time, magpies used to be pure white in color.

Soon Raven and the magpies came to a river and saw Salmon playing in the water. Salmon seemed to be having a very good time, but Raven wanted to cook Salmon for supper.

"Say there, Salmon," Raven called, "why don't you come closer to shore so we can play games with you?"

"No way," said Salmon. "We salmon know all about your tricks, Raven. We were not born yesterday, and I am not going to fall for your tricks. You just want to catch me!" Then Salmon darted quickly onto the shore and knocked the trickster so hard he fell unconscious. When Raven woke, he was angry at Salmon.

When Raven recovered, he dug a series of holes along the shoreline and flew away. When Salmon saw the holes the trickster had made, he decided to make a new game, jumping from one hole to the other. He did not know that Raven had snuck back and hidden himself in the last hole. When Salmon jumped into the last hole, Raven caught him. Then Raven lit a big fire, and prepared to cook Salmon for supper.

"Go and get me some big leaves to serve as plates," he told his nephews, the magpies. The magpies set out to get some leaves close by, but Raven told them that he wanted bigger plates and they could only be found further away. "Go and find them," he ordered.

When the magpies were gone, and Salmon was cooked, Raven devoured the fish except for the tail. He left the tail sticking out of a basket to make it look like Salmon was still in the basket. When the magpies looked into the basket and found that there was only the tail to eat, they got angry. Raven quickly threw ashes on the magpies and they immediately turned partly black. The magpies objected loudly. Raven warned them that did not stop their chattering, he would do something else to them. that stopped them.

From that day to this, magpies are black and white in color.

And now you know why.

Coyote and Water Serpent

A Hopi Legend

A LONG TIME AGO, Coyote, the trickster, and Water Serpent were very good friends. When they were quite young, they often visited one another in their lodges.

As time went on, they both grew older and bigger. In fact, one day Water Serpent grew so big he could hardly fit into his lodge. When Coyote visited him, there was hardly any room for Coyote to fit into Water Serpent's lodge.

Water Serpent was proud of his size and kept boasting about how large he was. All he could talk about was his size. He was so large and scary that he did not have to fear other animals.

"Am I not a remarkable size?" he would brag to Coyote. He said this so often that Coyote got quite tired of hearing it. As time went on, Coyote did not enjoy visiting Water Serpent anymore. There was no room for him in Water Serpent's home.

It was very humiliating for poor Coyote to see Water Serpent so large that he filled up his whole lodge. Whenever Coyote visited Water Serpent's house he had to scrunch up in one small corner. Water Serpent kept right on bragging. "Wouldn't you like to be as big as I am?" he taunted. One day Coyote had had enough. He decided to do something about it. Coyote had a few tricks up his sleeve.

Coyote decided to make his tail so large that by itself it would be as big as Water Serpent himself. Coyote went home and tried some of his magic tricks.

First, he rubbed different medicines on his tail, but they did nothing. Then he did some exercises, but his tail did not grow any larger. While he was looking for other solutions he noticed a large, thick branch of a cedar tree nearby. It occurred to him that he might be able to attach the cedar branch to his tail and make it appear larger. Maybe that way he could fool Water Serpent.

Coyote went to work, and covered the cedar branch with his own hair. Then he attached it to his body. Now it looked like it was his tail. Coyote brushed his new tail until it looked big and shiny. In fact, it was almost as large as Water Serpent. Coyote could hardly wait to see Water Serpent's face when he showed him his big tail.

The next day Coyote went to Water Serpent's lodge and showed off his huge tail. Water Serpent welcomed him and the two talked for a while, but Water Serpent did not say anything about Coyote's new tail. Coyote spent a lot of time coiling up his tail, but Water Serpent acted like he never noticed.

The next day Water Serpent went to Coyote's lodge but did not tell Coyote he was coming. Coyote saw him coming, and quickly attached his new tail. Coyote got his tail on just in time, and when Water Serpent tried to enter Coyote's lodge, there was no room for him. Coyote's tail took up all the space in the lodge.

As time went on, the two friends kept on visiting one another and showing off to one another. One day, however, something happened. Coyote's beautiful tail caught fire in Water Serpent's fireplace and Coyote did not notice it. When he left Water Serpent's lodge he discovered to his horror that there was fire and smoke behind him. He ran quickly because he thought he was being chased by fire. The fire was really Coyote's his own burning tail behind him and he did not even know it. Wherever he went the fire followed him.

Quickly the trickster scurried over to the river and plunged in. He tried frantically to swim across, but the weight of his wet tail dragged him downstream with the current. Soon he was dragged down beneath the river to the underworld where he was then forced to make his home.

Coyote and Water Serpent never visited one another again.

And now you know why.

Coyote and Wild Turkey
An Algonquian Legend

COYOTE, the trickster, was particularly fond of wild turkey meat. The problem was that he was hardly ever able to catch a wild turkey. The bird was simply too fast for him. Coyote tried many times to trap a wild turkey, but he was rarely able to do so.

One day Coyote came up with a devious plan. He rolled himself in a colorful blanket and rolled right over to where Wild Turkey was eating.

"I am having so much fun just rolling around in my bright blanket," Coyote said. "Would you like to play me? Come over and join the fun."

Without thinking, Wild Turkey crawled into the rolled up blanket with the Coyote. The trickster quickly tied the ends of the blanket so Wild Turkey could not get away.

After Wild Turkey had rolled around with the trickster for a while he began to understand what Coyote was up to. Wild Turkey said to Coyote. "I think I have had enough fun for today. Let's let some of those young turkeys over there have some fun too."

Coyote thought this was a good idea. That way he would have more than one turkey to roast for dinner. As soon as Coyote opened the ends of the blanket, Wild Turkey jumped out and ran away. He ran so fast that Coyote was unable to catch him.

Coyote quickly called out to the young turkeys to join him in his colorful blanket. "Come and join in the fun," he cried. "Wild Turkey and I had a great time. Come and let's start rolling around in my blanket."

One young turkey got into the blanket with Coyote, but Coyote thought he needed more than just one young turkey for supper so he called to the others. "Come and join the game. There is plenty of room for all of you."

After some coaxing, several young turkeys got onto the blanket and Coyote rolled it up. He quickly tied the ends of the blanket so the turkeys could not get out. Then he rolled the young turkeys over to his house and called to his wife that he had turkey meat for supper. When Mrs. Coyote saw the young wild turkeys she got very excited. In her excitement she quickly opened both ends of the blanket roll and all of the turkeys ran away as fast as they could.

Poor Coyote; now he would have to look elsewhere for his supper!

And now you know why.

Napi, Skunk, and the Prairie Dogs

A Blackfoot Legend

NAPI, THE TRICKSTER, was looking for something to eat when he came upon a village of prairie dogs. Napi liked prairie dog meat so he made up a clever plan to satisfy his appetite.

He went over to the prairie dogs asked them to join in a game he had invented. The game went something like this. Everyone was to dance in a circle with their eyes closed. Once the game started, Napi announced that if anyone opened their eyes during the dance something bad would happen to them.

The prairie dogs joined in the game, probably because they did not know about Napi's tricky ways. As soon as the dance started and all the prairie dogs closed their eyes shut, Napi grabbed a prairie dog, killed it, and set it aside for his supper. He told the prairie dogs to keep dancing and not to open their eyes lest something bad would happen to them. He kept right on grabbing the prairie dogs one by one and killing them.

As the game went on, one prairie dog *did* open his eyes and immediately realized that Napi was killing off his friends, one by one. Quickly this prairie dog shouted, "Run for your burrows. Napi is killing us."

The prairie dogs scurried to their dens before Napi could kill any more of them. Since he still had several prairie dogs left, the trickster set about roasting the ones he had killed.

In the meantime, Skunk had been watching Napi and laughing at the poor trusting prairie dogs who had fallen for Napi's trick. He helped Napi gather wood to roast the prairie dogs.

While the prairie dogs were cooking, Napi decided he wanted the best ones for himself. He spoke to Skunk, "Let us have a race and whoever wins gets first pick of the prairie dogs."

"That's not fair," said Skunk, "you would win easily since you are a fast runner. I could never keep up to you."

"Okay," said Napi. "to make the race fair, I will tie a large rock to my foot and also give you a head start." Skunk agreed, but he did not trust Napi so he made a plan of his own.

The two racers set off, but as soon as Skunk was out of sight, Napi untied the rock from his foot so he could outrun Skunk. In the meantime, Skunk had gone ahead, but hid behind a bush to see what Napi was up to. Soon he saw Napi running past without the rock tied his foot. Quickly Skunk went back to eat the roasted prairie dogs. He ate all of the prairie dogs except two skinny ones. He left those for Napi.

When Napi came back to the fire with great anticipation he reached into the ashes to find the roasted prairie dogs, but all he found were the two skinny ones that Skunk had left behind. Angry that he had been beaten at his own game, Napi glanced up and saw crafty Skunk sitting on top of a nearby hill, watching.

"This is not fair," Napi called out. "You took all the delicious prairie dogs. The only ones left are these two skinny ones. Give me some good ones."

In answer, Skunk threw down the bones of the prairie dogs he had eaten. "I beat you in the race, Napi," he cried. "Enjoy the two prairie dogs I left for you." Then he ran off.

Napi realized that Skunk was a better trickster than Napi himself! He never challenged Skunk again.

And now you know why.

Raven Burns a Canoe
A West Coast Legend

RAVEN, the trickster, sometimes played mean tricks on animals and people. For example, one day a young boy named Little Bow decided to make his own canoe.

His plan was to select a log, and hollow it out with his stone axe. Next he would build a fire and let it burn until only hot embers were left. Then he would place the live coals into the log and finish burning out the insides with live coals. Little Bow had seen his father and grandfather do this a number of times so he decided to do this for himself.

After searching around in the forest for a while Little Bow came upon a log that he thought would make a perfect canoe. With much effort he managed to drag the log into the village and began carving it into a canoe. Some of the villagers watched him with great interest. How could such a young boy manage to do such a difficult task?

Little Bow ignored the people who were watching and set to work. First, he took his stone axe and chopped into the log to make its insides hollow. It was hard work for a small boy, but Little Bow was determined to get the job done. After cutting away some of the inside wood to hollow the log, Little Bow was ready to burn out the rest of the canoe. He built a fire and waited until its embers were red hot. Then he took a shovel and put some of the hot embers into the log. He sat down and waited for them to burn away the inside of the log.

As Little Bow worked he did not notice that a stranger had come close by to watch him. It was Raven, the trickster, disguised as a man. Little Bow ignored Raven until Raven started to sing and dance. He was such a good dancer that Little Bow began to watch him. He said to himself. "I wish I could dance that well. I wonder if the stranger would teach me."

Suddenly Little Bow smelled smoke. He turned around and saw his canoe on fire. He had become so engrossed in watching Raven dance that he forgot to remove the embers from his canoe. Now the canoe was burning, and soon only ashes were left.

Raven watched all of this with great amusement, then stopped dancing and went off laughing.

And now you know what happened to Little Bow's canoe.

Raven Learns a Lesson
A Tsimshian Legend

RAVEN, the trickster, was hungry. In fact, it seemed as though he was always hungry, but he was just a bit too lazy to hunt for food. Raven preferred to have others do his hunting for him. He also liked to use tricks to get his food from others. Now he was so hungry he decided to go to a nearby village and find some food.

As Raven neared the village, he saw smoke coming out of the smoke hole of a lodge so he knew that someone must have been cooking something. After all, it was getting close to dinnertime.

As soon as the villagers saw Raven coming, someone called, "A stranger is coming. A stranger is coming."

The chief of the village welcomed Raven and invited him into his lodge for supper. Raven was very pleased.

As the meal got underway, Raven was surprised that no one had to serve him. Every dish seemed to come to the table with no one carrying it. First, Raven saw a beautifully carved box open itself and a salmon came out of it: ready to be cooked. Next, a nice dish filled itself with salmon and went over to the fire and began to cook the salmon. Then the dish came over to Raven and set itself down in front of him.

Raven was astonished at this magic. This must be an important chief to have so much power. Quickly Raven ate the salmon.

Next, a large bowl of crabapples with a spoon in the bowl came over to Raven and set itself down in front of him. Raven ate all the crabapples, and then a bowl of cranberries arrived. Raven ate everything in sight and started to develop a plan.

Raven saw a huge piece of mountain goat meat hanging from a hook on the dining wall, and decided to take it home with him when he left. That way he would have food for the next day. He knew he would have to take the mountain goat meat in a hurry because someone might just see what he was up to.

When he thought no one was looking, Raven grabbed the mountain goat meat and struck for the door. Suddenly, a large stone hammer came out of nowhere and hit Raven on the ankle. Raven was in severe pain and could hardly walk after that. Quickly, he dropped the mountain goat meat and slowly limped back to his lodge.

Raven could hear people laughing at him behind his back. He never visited that village again.

And now you know why.

The Trickster and Eagle
An Assiniboine Legend

IKTÛMNI, the trickster, decided he wanted to make a war bonnet using eagle feathers, but he did not have any eagle feathers.

As he continued to plan, Iktûmni saw Eagle flying above him and decided to obtain some feathers from him.

Iktûmni called out to Eagle. "Come here, my brother Eagle. I am glad I saw you. I want to talk to you. You are such a good looking bird I would enjoy talking with you."

At first Eagle was hesitant, but Iktûmni kept on complimenting Eagle so he finally flew down and landed on the ground before Iktûmni. "What did you want to talk to me about?" Eagle asked.

"Oh, I just wanted to pass the time of day with you," the trickster said. "It is always nice to be with a good looking bird such as yourself." Eagle liked Iktûmni's words and kept listening.

While Iktûmni was talking to Eagle he was busy pulling feathers out of Eagle's tail. Eagle did not notice until it was too late. Suddenly he noticed that all of his tail feathers were gone. Now he would not be able to fly.

Iktûmni pushed Eagle away and said, "Go away. Now I have enough feathers to build my war bonnet. You can just go away." He gave Eagle another push and made him stumble as he walked away. Poor Eagle had to wait a very long time before his tail feathers grew back and he could fly again. In the meantime he had to walk everywhere.

Eagle was determined to punish the trickster for what he had done. Four months later, when he was finally able to fly again, Eagle flew quietly over to where Iktûmni was and picked him up by the shoulders with his sharp claws. Iktûmni screamed in pain, but Eagle would not listen. There was no one to help Iktûmni, because no one could fly as high as Eagle.

    Eagle flew high into the sky with Iktûmni, and eventually came to a very tall tree. Then Eagle said to Iktûmni. "I am going to drop you over the longest branch of that tall tree. Be sure to hang onto the branch when I let you go." Iktûmni screamed and begged for mercy, but Eagle would not listen.

Eagle let Iktûmni drop and the trickster managed to grab onto the branch that Eagle had pointed out. Iktûmni hung onto the branch for a long time until his arms got tired. His eyes began to swell from crying, and he was sure his arms were getting longer.

    Finally he had to let go of the branch and fell down into a muddy swamp. He was completely covered with warm, oozy mud, but slowly he managed to make his way to dry land. Then he dried off and went on to his next adventure. Iktûmni, the trickster, never bothered Eagle again.

    And now you know why.

Appendices

Appendix A
A Note on Terminology

Readers may wonder at the choice of terminology for this book's title, and we did give the matter serious thought. There is, in fact, a wide variety of descriptive terms to choose from in writing about the original occupants of this continent, and there seems to be no front-runner. One can choose from a long list of descriptors: Aboriginal People, AmerIndians, First Nations, First People, Indians, Indigenous Peoples, Native Americans, Native American Indians, and North American Indians. There are writers, Native and nonNative, who prefer a particular usage to the exclusion of all others. Currently the Government of the United States, and American writers, use the terms "Indian," or "Native Americans," while Canadians are opting for First Nations, Indigenous People, or Aboriginals. The Government of Canada still operates a Department of Indian and Northern Affairs.

Despite arguments to the contrary, in our writings we prefer to employ a variety of terms, partly to relieve monotony in delivery, and partially because it is difficult to know which usage might be appropriate in a given context. Sadly, it seems that today writers have been stymied in word choice because the political correctness movement has stalled efforts at meaningful literary communication. Being too fussy about word usage can confine or even close off completely the scope of investigation, ensuring that whatever "truth" emerges will be partial at best. In this volume, words to describe the First Peoples are capitalized as a means of emphasizing the literary legitimacy of writing about the AmerIndians, in the same way that identities of other nationalities are capitalized.

Appendix B
Interpreting Legends

BEFORE THE EUROPEANS arrived in North America, Native American Indian societies were particularly adept at preserving cultural knowledge through legends and stories. Today, both Canadian and American readers are very fortunate in being able to access Native legends in written form which offer special insights to a way of life that dominated this continent for many centuries. Appreciation for the preservation of these tales must be extended to several sectors, particularly elders who took upon themselves the responsibility of maintaining the essence of the oral tradition during times when their people were under siege to abandon traditional ways. These guardians of revered knowledge have been successful in keeping many of their valued beliefs and practices alive through very culturally turbulent times. Adherents to the written word who first came into contact with Indigenous cultures – traders, missionaries, settlers, anthropologists, and Indian agents (who appeared later) – also rendered a valuable service by committing to writing many stories they learned from their new-found acquaintances.

Stories preserved by the original inhabitants of this continent have a unique identity. They are original to this continent, and as such they constitute the oral literature of the many Native American Indian tribal cultural configurations. First Nations (the current preferred term in Canada) stories are pictures of Aboriginal life verbally sketched by Indigenous storytellers, showing life from their point of view. Legends deal with spirituality, the origins of things, and various kinds of individual behavior. Legends are often entertaining and they may convey a vast range of cultural knowledge including folkways, values, and beliefs.

The study of Native legends can be a very rich source of learning. Traditionally, legends appear to have been told for a variety of purposes, both formal and informal. Formal storytelling was usually connected to the occasion of deliberate moral, cultural, or spiritual instruction. Some legends were considered so sacred that their telling was restricted to the celebration of a very special event such as the Sundance. Others were told only during specific seasons. On these occasions, only recognized or designated persons could engage in their telling. Nearly anyone could engage in informal storytelling, and such legends were usually related for their entertainment or instructional value.

It is possible to classify Native legends into four categories (with some degree of overlap), each of which has a special purpose. Entertainment legends, for example, are often about the trickster: a fictional character with magical powers. He is known by a variety of names among the various tribes. For example, the Blackfoot/Blackfeet call him Napi, the Crees call him Wisakedjak, the Ojibway call him Nanabush, the Sioux call him Iktûmni, and other tribes have different names for him like Coyote, Saynday, Tarantula, or Raven. Stories about the trickster are principally fictional and can be invented and amended during the very process of storytelling.

Trickster stories often involve playing tricks. Sometimes the trickster plays tricks on others and sometimes they play tricks on him. The trickster usually has the advantage over his unsuspecting audience, however, since he possesses supernatural powers, which he deploys on a whim to startle or to shock. He has powers to raise animals to life and he himself may even die and in four days come to life again. Aside from being amusing, trickster stories often incorporate knowledge about aspects of Aboriginal culture, buffalo hunts, natural phenomena, rituals, or the relationship between people and animals. In this sense, trickster stories can also be instructional.

A second category of Native stories may be called instructional or teaching legends, which are told for the purpose of sharing information about a tribe's culture, history, or origin. These stories explain things. They often use animal motifs to explain why things are the way they are. A child may inquire about the origin of the seasons or the creation of the world, and a tale about animal life may be told. For example, a child may ask, "Why do rabbits change color with the seasons?" or "Why are magpies' feathers black and white?" Stories told in response to these questions could include adventures of the trickster. The legends contained in this volume are instructional in the sense that they all answer questions that begin with "how or why." As a bonus we have chosen to include ten entertaining "tricky trickster tales" at the end of this volume.

Parallel with the practice of traditionally oriented cultures of the past, the First People of North America were concerned about teaching their offspring the difference between right and wrong behavior. To fulfill this purpose, a third category of stories known as moral legends were invented to teach ideal or "right" forms of behavior. These legends were related to suggest to the listener that a change in attitude or action would be desirable.

Since traditional Indian tribes rarely corporally punished their children, they sometimes found it useful to hint at the inappropriateness of certain behavior by telling stories. For example, the story might be about an animal friend who engages in inappropriate behavior and the hearer is expected to realize that a possible modification of his or her own behavior is the object of the telling.

Only a recognized elder or other tribal approved individual traditionally told sacred or spiritual legends, which comprise a fourth type of legend, and their telling was considered a form of worship. Tribal origin stories were often included in this category. More recently many origin stories have found their way into print, published by both Aboriginal and nonAboriginal writers.

Naturally, cultural stories used to comprise only a part of a Native American tribe's spiritual structure, which also included ceremonies, rituals, songs, and dances. Physical objects such as fetishes, pipes, painted tepee designs, medicine bundles, and shrines of sorts supplemented these activities.

Familiarity with these components comprised sacred knowledge, and everything learned was committed to memory. Viewed together, these entries represented spiritual connections between people and the universe, which, with appropriate care, resulted in a lifestyle of assured food supply, physical well-being and the satisfaction of other societal needs.

Appendix C

Native American Rock Art: Pictographs and Petroglyphs

THE ILLUSTRATIONS IN THIS BOOK represent a very ancient and studied form of art called rock art, which consist of pictographs and petroglyphs. Traditionally, various Native Americans created unique styles of this form of art with distinguishing marks unique to each tribe. The illustrations in this book are therefore generic, but provide an indication of basic fundamental forms. Today scientists are devoting considerable attention to differentiating various tribal styles, as well as trying to decipher the meanings of the ancient symbols. Some of the more common rock art symbols appear to be related to tribal migrations, clan designations, maps, astronomical interpretations, and spirituality. The following section offers a brief sketch of the historical background to the study of pictographs and petroglyphs. The purpose of including these representations in this book was to add substance to the message of the legends and give audience to a rich cultural dimension of North America's original inhabitants.

Nature of Rock Art

PICTOGRAPHS AND PETROGLYPHS are probably the oldest form of Indigenous art. Both of these art forms can be identified throughout North America on vertical cliffs, rock shelters, boulders, and flat rock surfaces. Pictographs are basically paintings of figures on rocks. Petroglyphs, which are more common than pictographs, are found on the dark, exposed surfaces of rock such as sandstone and basalt. Petroglyphs were created by an individual scratching, scraping, grinding, or pecking the rock. However, both pictographs and petroglyphs lend themselves to a solid or outline technique. Pecking into the rock to create petroglyphs was traditionally accomplished with a hammerstone or chisel, basically creating a preliminary outline of the figure. Different pecking techniques exhibited different styles. Incising or scratching with a sharp tool was also done. Incised designs were more expressive and detailed than pecked designs.

Pictographs were usually painted on rock surfaces using only one color with pigments made from a variety of elements, such as soot or powdered minerals, and made permanent by being covered with blood, eggs, animal fat, plant juice, or urine. The colors generally used were red, white, black, and orange, and less often green, blue, and turquoise. Red pigment probably came from hematite or iron oxide; orange was created from a combination of hematite and limonite. Malachite provided the green, azurite the blue, and turquoise probably came from ground up turquoise. Other sources of pigment included white clay, silica, gypsum, chalk, calcium carbonate, and charcoal. Pastels were created from clay mixed with other minerals. Created forms were often representational in the shape of humans, animals, plants, weapons, teepees, real objects, or celestial bodies. Archaeological estimates suggest that these art forms may be as many as 25 000 years old, and were produced by nomadic gatherers and hunters of the past. Many contemporary Aboriginal artists have been inspired by these images and have attempted to decipher their often hidden meanings.

Rock art formations provide a hint of fascinating stories behind each scene, and researchers feel fortunate in having many such sites available for exploration. It is fortunate for rock art enthusiasts that more than 1200 sites remain in the Northwest including Alberta, Saskatchewan, Montana, Wyoming and the Dakotas. The southwest United States is also home to dozens of ancient rock art sites. Unfortunately, however, many sites in these areas have been lost or deliberately destroyed over the years.

Often located near awesome natural scenes of beauty, rock art forms were created to reflect a deep respect for the mystery of nature, which was viewed as charged with spiritual energy. Ethnographic, archaeological, and historic records are replete with references to visions, offerings, and burials at such places. There is also evidence that imagination was a potent force in the conceptual thinking of the prehistoric peoples. For example, many of the paleolithic sketches of human forms were not in any way exact likenesses, and did not delineate facial features. They were purely creative and imaginative, not representative forms. This indicates that human portrayals, particularly female forms, were carefully overemphasized or deemphasized as a means of projecting more imaginative forms.

Purpose of Rock Art

IT HAS BEEN SPECULATED that rock art was originally created for a variety of purposes: aesthetic, magical, religious, historical, astronomical, as a part of hunting rituals, or a combination of the above. Many First Nations regard rock art sites as sacred places, since some of them were designed for ceremonial purposes such as puberty and fertility rites, pre-hunting rituals, weather control, and possibly healing ceremonies. Many sites chronicle the long histories, hunting ceremonies, and religions of the region's First Peoples. Some Aboriginal authorities posit that rock art was traditionally perceived as having originated in the spirit world. Since the Indigenous people believed that everything in life represented a celestial order, all objects and beings were seen as having sacred spiritual powers. This perspective has sometimes been difficult for nonAboriginal researchers to appreciate. As a result, rock art has often been misunderstood. It is now realized that interpretations that consider Indigenous metaphysics allow for knowledge flow that is not obtainable anywhere else.

Some observers have speculated that ancient rock art was primarily used as an aid to memory. Indigenous healers, for example, would carve signs to indicate the location of medicinal plants in order to remember where the plants were when they needed them. Woodland Indians, for example, used small indicators carved on rock to indicate tribally important locations. While most rock art, like other Aboriginal art forms, had spiritual or cosmological implications, other purposes included recording significant historical events. Ojibway men, for example, tended to carve war clubs that had explicit images of military and spiritual biographies. Plains warriors recorded visionary experiences on war shields made of double buffalo hides as permanent reminders of heroic deeds or battle honors. Visions were powerful motivators for a variety of behaviors. A Paiute prophet named Wovoka had visions that led to the origin of the Ghost Dance. He promised that performances of the dance would bring about the return of the buffalo and resurrect the traditional Indian way of life. The western magpie was Wovoka's spirit guardian.

Rock Art Sites

AMONG THE BEST-KNOWN rock art sites in North America is Writing-on-Stone Provincial Park in southern Alberta. Here, hundreds of petroglyphs, as well as some pictographs, are located on sandstone bluffs and spread along some twenty miles (thirty kilometers) or so on the Milk River. Blackfoot elders say that individuals used to go to this site for vision questing. According to tribal lore, one respected shaman went there to commune with the spirits about the future. As has been observed with regard to Writing-on-Stone Provincial Park, individuals with artistic inclinations were sometimes inspired to create their drawings by resident spirits. To commemorate a successful vision, the seeker might give thanks to the spirit world and perhaps paint a pictograph of the guardian spirit or other dream subjects. One elder who visited the Writing-on-Stone-Provincial Park site reported getting the power to hunt from a deer and the power to gamble from the experience. The best-portrayed scene at Writing-on-Stone is the battle scene. It may have been recorded after the battle between Peigans and Gros Ventre. Some say it may have been put there before the battle as a warning to the Peigans.

Another Canadian rock art site of interest is the Peterborough Petroglyphs, located near the City of Peterborough, Ontario, and discovered by anthropologists in 1962. This site dates the beginning of Canada's Aboriginal art history. Recently the site has become an international attraction, motivating authorities to erect a covered building to protect the site from damage and natural decay. The most distinctive scenes at this site are narratives describing battles and other activities recorded in graphic detail. Images of carts, horses, and rifles give evidence of the continuity of rock art well into the post-contact period.

The American southwest is also home to a myriad of outstanding rock art sites, many of them traceable to the Anazasi and Hohokam cultures of 2000 years ago. Four exemplary sites include Petroglyph National Monument at Albuquerque, New Mexico, Mojave River Petroglyphs in Barstow, California, Painted Rock Petroglyph Site, located west of Gila Bend, Arizona, and Parowan Gap, which is near Cedar City, Utah. Petroglyph National Monument contains more than 15 000 prehistoric images stretching some seventeen miles along

Albuquerque's West Mesa escarpment, documenting at least 12 000 years of human occupation in the area.

The Mojave River site in Barstow, California contains dozens of human, animal, geometric, and environmental figures that document the same time period.

The Painted Rock Petroglyph site in Arizona is of Hohokam origin, and consists of forty sites, one of which, the Painted Rock Site, features over 800 images. The Hohokam people once lived and farmed in the Gila Bend area. Ruins of their late Pioneer Period (AD 350-AD 550) and Early Colonial Period (AD 550-AD 700) villages are found to the north and west, and ruins of their Sedentary-Classic Period (AD 900-AD 1400) villages are found to the south and east. Parowan Gap in Utah is thought to be of Anasazi origin, and its north wall contains a huge gallery of Native American rock art. Most of the site images are figures of humans and animals and deeply inscribed geometric forms. The most interesting feature of this site is a very large and deeply inscribed petroglyph known as the "Zipper," which many archaeologists believe to be a composite map of space and a numerical calendar of time.

Types of Rock Art

ARCHAEOLOGICAL EXPERTS have identified two basic types of rock art, distinguished by such characteristics as subject matter, forms used to illustrate subjects, compositional relationships, techniques used to produce designs, and specific landscape setting. Techniques used to date rock art include association with dated archaeological deposits, that is, sometimes a piece of rock art may have fallen off and appears to be older than the materials burying it. Sometimes rock art may be associated with dated portable artifacts or art, and sometimes the same design may be placed on a rock panel as well as on a nearby portable object that can be dated. At times it is possible to date portable items (like weapons), introduced by incoming Europeans, and use them as a base by which to date nonportable rock art. Also, if a number of certain designs are consistently superimposed on a piece of rock, a generalized chronology may be implied.

Scientists sometimes use patination and weathering to date rock art. For example, when a petroglyph is pecked or incised, it exposes a lighter color stone beneath it, and the rock varnish may slowly reappear. Over time the design may become repatinated so that it is changed to the same color as the unaltered rock face. It is sometimes possible to date rock art with chronometric methods such as radiocarbon dating, which measures the radioactivity decay of unstable carbon isotope relative to its stable isotope, accelerator mass spectrometry, and location ratio dating. The subjects of the art may provide another method of dating. For example, if a horse is represented, the rock art is from the 16th century or later, because Spaniards imported horses to the New World beginning in the 1500s.

Anthropologists who first interpreted rock art produced descriptive studies, because no one knew what else to do with them. Original EuroAmerican speculations ranged from the notion that petroglyphs were mere doodles executed to relieve boredom, to the arbitrary application of a host of weird religious or superstitious speculations. Some early observers perceived them as maps of buried treasure, or diagrams of astronomical phenomena, or regarded them as proof of the existence of foreign language groups. Consultation with AmerIndian elders about rock art has been undertaken only recently and resultant interpretations have been quite different. Now, thanks to increased faith in the oral tradition and the assistance of Native elders, it has become possible to decipher some degree of function or meaning from rock art. As it turns out, using inferences from known pieces, it has been deduced that most rock art depicts traditional explanations for images, and relationships between rock art and other aspects of human nature. A more difficult challenge is to determine the underlying dynamics of the belief system that influenced these creations.

A Diminishing Art

By the 1860s, Aboriginal rock art became a vanishing art form. Plains Indian men tended to resort to use of ledgers or account books that they had traded for or found through some source to record important events. Aboriginal women gradually entered this domain and began putting pictographic illustrations in their beadwork designs. By the 1890s, portrayals of cultural and ceremonial life began to appear, many of them produced by young people who were not familiar with traditional historical happenings. The plains winter count, a pictorial expression of naming the years from winter to winter, was suddenly portrayed in various art forms. For example, an entry might be, "I was born the year of the last buffalo hunt." Then, as though nothing was considered too sacred any more, even the Sundance was recorded in beadwork. Afraid that their traditional beliefs and art forms would be lost when the reserve system was established, many Native artists began to use pictographs to preserve accounts for succeeding generations. On occasion such drawings were even commissioned by Indian agents and their sale brought necessary funds to needy families. This practice set the stage for the new genre of Aboriginal art that was to follow.

As the twenty-first century unfolds, public interest in Native American Indian history and cultural life continues to intensify, accompanied with the hope that observers will expand their interests to the examination of archaic rock art. These formations comprise a rich source of information about the spirituality and artistic inclinations of North America's First Peoples. Hopefully our efforts, and the graciousness of Detselig Publishers in putting this volume into print, will complement that objective.

Appendix D:
About the Authors

JOHN W. FRIESEN, Ph.D., D.Min., D.R.S., is a Professor in the Graduate Division of Educational Research Education at the University of Calgary, where he teaches courses in Aboriginal history and education. An ordained clergyman with the All Native Circle Conference of the United Church of Canada, he is the recipient of three eagle feathers, and author, co-author, or editor of more than fifty books including:

Rose of the North (a novel), (Borealis, 1987);

Introduction to Teaching: A Socio-Cultural Approach (with Alice L. Boberg), (Kendall/Hunt, 1990);

You Can't Get There From Here: The Mystique of North American Plains Indians Culture & Philosophy (Kendall/Hunt, 1995);

The Real/Riel Story: An Interpretive History of the Métis People of Canada (Borealis, 1996);

Perceptions of the Amish Way (with Bruce K. Friesen) (Kendall/Hunt, 1996);

Rediscovering the First Nations of Canada (Detselig, 1997);

Sayings of the Elders: An Anthology of First Nations' Wisdom (Detselig, 1998);

First Nations of the Plains: Creative, Adaptable and Enduring (Detselig, 1999);

Legends of the Elders (Detselig, 2000);

Aboriginal Spirituality and Biblical Theology: Closer Than You Think, (Detselig, 2000);

Canada in the Twenty-First Century: A Historical Sociological Approach (with Trevor W. Harrison), (Pearson Canada, 2004);

The Palgrave Companion to Utopian Communities in North America (with Virginia Lyons Friesen), (Macmillan, 2004);

Sayings of a Philosopher (Detselig, 2005); and,

What's Your Church Like? Compared to Nine New Testament Models (with Virginia Lyons Friesen) (Xulon, 2007).

VIRGINIA LYONS FRIESEN, Ph.D., is a Sessional Instructor in the Faculty of Communication and Culture at the University of Calgary and is an instructor at Weekend University, University of Calgary Gifted Centre, and Old Sun College on the Blackfoot Indian Reserve at Siksika, Alberta. An Early Childhood Education Specialist, she holds a Certificate in Counseling from the Institute of Pastoral Counseling in Akron, Ohio. She has co-presented a number of papers at academic conferences and is co-author of:

Grade Expectations: A Multicultural Handbook for Teachers, (Alberta Teachers' Association 1995);

The Palgrave Companion to Utopian Communities in North America (Macmillan, 2004); and,

What's Your Church Like? Compared to Nine New Testament Models (Xulon, 2007).

She served as Director of Christian Education with the Morley United Church on the Stoney (Nakoda Sioux) Indian Reserve from 1988 to 2001, and from 2007 to 2008.

JOHN W. FRIESEN and VIRGINIA LYONS FRIESEN have co-authored the following Detselig Titles:

In Defense of Public Schools in North America, 2001;

Aboriginal Education in Canada: A Plea for Integration, 2002;

We Are Included: The Métis People of Canada Realize Riel's Vision, (2004);

More Legends of the Elders, (2004);

First Nations in the Twenty-First Century: Contemporary Educational Frontiers, 2005;

Still More Legends of the Elders, 2005;

Even More Legends of the Elders 2005;

Teachers' Guide to Legends of the Elders, 2005;

Canadian Aboriginal Art and Spirituality: A Vital Link, 2006; and,

Western Canadian Native Destiny: The Cultural Maze Revisited, 2008.

The Friesens' website is drsfriesen.artdesignlife.com.

About the Artist

An apprenticed blacksmith, DAVID J FRIESEN studied design at the Alberta College of Art and obtained a Bachelor of Education degree in Early Childhood Education from the University of Calgary. He has taught elementary and art education in both public and private schools in Alberta, British Columbia, Ohio, Korea, and Japan. His interests include skateboarding, skimboarding, music, and web and graphic design.

Bibliography

The legends contained in this volume have been drawn from the following sources. They have been summarized, edited, and adapted to render them suitable for children's reading level.

Bemister, Margaret. (1973). *Thirty Indian Legends of Canada.* Vancouver, BC: Douglas & McIntyre, 134-137, 145-148.

Blackburn, Thomas C. (1975). *December's Child: A Book of Chumash Oral Narratives.* Berkeley, CA: University of Berkeley Press, 95.

Brown, Dee. (1993). Dee Brown's *Folktales of the Native American: Retold for Our Times.* New York: Henry Holt and Company, 111-113.

Bruchac, Joseph. (1993). *The Native American Sweatlodge: History and Legends.* Freedom, CA: The Crossing Press, 54-56.

Burland, Cottie. (1975). *North American Indian Mythology.* London, UK: Paul Hamlyn, 65.

Clark, Ella. (1988). *Indian Legends From the Northern Rockies.* Norman, OK: University of Oklahoma Press, 98-100, 270-273.

Clark, Ella. (1971). *Indian Legends of Canada.* Toronto, ON: McClelland and Stewart, 80.

Clutesi, George. (1967). *Son of Raven, Son of Deer: Fables of the Tse-shaht People.* Vancouver, BC: Gray's Publishing Ltd., 39-43.

Curtis, Natalie. (1987). *The Indians' Book: Authentic Native American Legends, Lore & Music.* New York: Bonanza Books, 12.

Dary, David A. (1990). *The Buffalo Book: The Full Saga of the American Animal*. Columbus, OH: Sage Books, Ohio University Press, 54-56.

Eastman, Charles A (Ohiyesa), and Elaine Goodale Eastman. 2001. *Wigwam Evenings: 27 Sioux Folk Tales*. Mineola, NY: Dover Publications, Inc., 8-9.

Edmonds, Margot, and Ella A. Clark. (1989). *Voices of the Winds: Native American Legends*. New York, NY: Facts on File, 212-213.

Erdoes, Richard, and Alfonso Ortiz, eds. (1984). *American Indian Myths and Legends*. New York: Pantheon Books, 356-357, 375-377.

Garbarino, Merwyn S., and Robert F. Sasso. (1994). *Native American Heritage*. Third edition. Prospect Heights, IL: Waveland Press, 324-335.

Gifford, Barry, ed. (1976). *Selected Writings of Edward S. Curtis: Excerpts from Volumes 1-XX of The North American Indian*. Berkeley, CA: Creative Arts Book Company, 8-9.

Grant, Agnes. (1990). *Our Bit of Truth: An Anthology of Canadian Native Literature*. Winnipeg, MB: Pemmican Publications, 18-10, 44-45.

Gunn, S. W. A. (1965). *The Totem Poles in Stanley Park: Vancouver, BC*. Second edition, B.C. Centenary Issue. Vancouver, BC: W. E. G. Macdonald, publisher, 18-19.

Hulpach, Vladimir. (1965). *American Indian tales and Legends*. London, UK: Paul Hamlyn, 89-92, 146-148.

Hungrywolf, Adolf. (2001). *Legends Told by the People of many Tribes*. Summertown, TN: Native Voices, 67-68.

Jones, David M., and Brian L. Molyneaux. (2004). *Mythology of the American Nations*. London, UK: Hermes House, 38-39.

Kirk, Ruth. (1986). *Wisdom of the Elders: Native Traditions on the Northwest Coast*. Vancouver, BC: Douglas & McIntyre, 82-83.

Krause, Aurel. (1971). *The Tlinget Indians: Results of a Trip to the Northwest Coast of America and the Bering Strait*. Seattle, WA: University of Washington Press, 181-182.

Levitas, Gloria, Frank Robert Vivelo, and Jacqueline J. Vivelo, eds. (1974). *American Indian Prose and Poetry: We Wait in the Darkness*. New York: G. P. Putnam's Sons, 39.

Macfarlan, Allan A., ed. (1968). *North American Indian Legends*. Mineola, NY: Dover Publications, Inc., 273-275, 291-292.

Macmillan, Cyrus. (1967). *Glooskap's Country and Other Indian Tales*. Toronto, ON: Oxford University Press, 35-40.

Marriott, Alice, and Carol K. Rachlin. (1975). *Plains Indian Mythology*. New York: New American Library, 67-68, 75-78.

Mayo, Gretchen Will. (1990). *North American Indian Stories*. New York: Walker and Company, 17-20.

McClintock, Walter. (1992). *The Old North Trail: Life, Legends and Religion of the Blackfeet Indians*. Lincoln, NE: University of Nebraska Press, 491-501.

McHugh, Tom. (1972). *The Time of the Buffalo*. Lincoln, NE: University of Nebraska Press, 148.

Mclean, John. (1889). *The Indians: Their Manners and Customs*. Toronto, ON: William Briggs. Reprinted by Coles Publishing Company in Toronto, Ontario, in 1970, 182.

Mourning Dove. (1990). *Coyote Stories*. Lincoln, NE: University of Nebraska Press, 135-137.

Mullett, G. M., ed. (1979). *Spider Woman Stories: Legends of the Hopi*. Tucson, AZ: The University of Arizona Press, 132-140.

Palmer, William R. (1946). *Pahute Indian Legends*. Salt Lake City, UT: Deseret Book Company, 119-123.

Penn, W.S., ed. (1990). *The Telling of the World: Native American Stories and Art*. New York: Stewart, Tabori & Chang, 42.

Radin, Paul. (1937). *The Story of the American Indian*. Garden City, NY: Garden City Publishing Co., Inc., 345-346.

Reese, Montana Lisle, State Supervisor. (1994). *Legends of the Mighty Sioux*. Interior, SD: Badlands Natural History Association, 67-68.

Ressler, Theodore Whitson. (1957). *Treasury of American Indian Tales*. New York: Bonanza Books, 89-95.

Robertson, Marion. (1969). *Red Earth: Tales of the Micmacs with an introduction to the customs and beliefs of the Micmac Indians*. Halifax, NS: Nimbus Publishing Ltd, 42.

Shaw, Anna Moore. (1992). *Pima Indian Legends*. Tucson, AZ: University of Arizona Press, 76-78.

Smith, Philip, ed. (1994). *Favorite North American Indian Legends*. New York: Dover Publications, 14-20.

Spence, Lewis. (1994). *North American Indians: Myths and Legends*. London, UK: George G. Harrap & Company Ltd, 268.

Steckley, John L., and Bryan D. Cummins. (2001). *Full Circle: Canada's First Nations*. Toronto, ON: Prentice-Hall, 3.

Stiffarm, Preston L., ed. (1983). *Assiniboine Memories*. Fort Belknap, MT: Fort Belknap Education Department, Fort Belknap Community Council, 127-129.

Tiet, James A. (1968). *Shuswap Coyote Stories. The North American Indians: A Sourcebook*. Owen, Roger C., James J. F. Deetz, and Anthony D. Fisher, eds. New York: Macmillan, 282.

Wallas, Chief James, as told to Pamela Whitaker. (1989). *Kwakiutl Legends*. Surrey, BC: Hancock House Publishers, Ltd., 82-84.

Weatherby, Hugh. (1944). *Tales Totems Tell*. Toronto, ON: The Macmillan Company, 29-39.

Wissler, Clark. (1966). *Indians of the United States*. Garden City, NY: Doubleday, 44.